Stepney Gaswor

The archaeology and
Commercial Gas Light and Coke Company's
works at Harford Street, London E1, 1837–1946

MOLA Archaeology Studies Series

For more information about these titles and other MOLA publications visit the publications page at www.museumoflondonarchaeology.org.uk

Stepney Gasworks

The archaeology and history
of the Commercial Gas Light
and Coke Company's works at
Harford Street, London E1, 1837–1946

Antony Francis

MOLA ARCHAEOLOGY STUDIES SERIES 22

MUSEUM OF LONDON ARCHAEOLOGY

Published by Museum of London Archaeology
Copyright © Museum of London 2010

A CIP catalogue record for this book is available from the British Library

Production and series design by Tracy Wellman
Typesetting and design by Sue Cawood
Reprographics by Andy Chopping
Copy editing by Katy Carter
Series editing by Sue Hirst/Susan M Wright

Printed by the Lavenham Press

*Front cover: a collar on the middle tier of girders of gasholder 1 (XI), bearing
the badge of the Commercial Company*

CONTRIBUTORS

Principal author	Antony Francis
Graphics	Catherine Drew, Jonathan Godfrey, Carlos Lemos, Kenneth Lymer, Joseph Severn
Photography	Edwin Baker, Maggie Cox
Project managers	David Lakin, David Bowsher
Editor	Bruno Barber
Academic adviser	Michael Bussell

CONTENTS

FIGURES

SUMMARY

In 2002, Museum of London Archaeology (MOLA) was commissioned to undertake a building recording survey of a 19th-century gasworks in Stepney, London E1. The gasworks had been the principal works of the Commercial Gas Light and Coke Company, set up in 1837. The surviving remains dated from the 1850s to the early 20th century, and included four gasholders, an elevated tramway and perimeter walls. This publication presents the results of the survey, integrated with a new documentary history of the Company.

The gasworks was located on the Regent's Canal to facilitate coal deliveries. It grew from one small gasholder, a retort house and a purifying house in 1839 to five large gasholders, four retort houses and a complex of purifying equipment by the end of the century. Twelve gasholders were built during the history of the gasworks. The Company supplied town gas to much of east London, including Stepney, Whitechapel, Bethnal Green,

Bow and Poplar.

The Commercial's first years were a struggle for survival against more powerful rivals. However, within a short time agreements over areas of supply had been made, and the Company received its Act of Incorporation in 1847. In the 1850s the Stepney Works underwent major reconstruction, providing a firm basis for the Company to deal with increasing legislation from 1860 and rising demand as the capital grew. The Company's relationship with its competitors was always fractious, sometimes leading to physical violence. There were also episodes of industrial unrest, particularly in 1872, which saw the Company's workforce join a London-wide strike.

Gas making ceased at Stepney in 1945 and the works closed in 1946. The site was then used as a gasholder station (for storage of gas produced elsewhere) by the nationalised North Thames Gas Board and its successors until the 1990s. Since then the site has been redeveloped for housing, but a number of historic features have been retained or reused within the development.

The Commercial Company's history and the development of its Stepney Works have not received the detailed attention they deserved until now. This publication restores the Company to its rightful place in the story of London's gas industry.

ACKNOWLEDGEMENTS

The building recording survey and historical research were funded by Bellway Homes Urban Renewal Southern (now Bellway Homes Ltd). The analysis and publication project were funded by Bellway Homes Ltd.

Special thanks are due to Mike Melly and Roger Bond of Bellway Homes Urban Renewal Southern who arranged access to the site and the necessary plant, and ensured that the fieldwork ran smoothly in the face of numerous difficulties. Victoria Bullock of Barton Willmore, Rob Carter and Vivien Fenyvesi of Merebrook Projects Ltd, and Jim Farrant of Tully De'Ath also provided valuable assistance.

The senior archaeologist during the fieldwork and pre-publication reporting and analysis was Kieron Tyler. On-site survey was undertaken by Jonathan Godfrey, Cordelia Hall and Joseph Severn of MOLA. The survey drawings were compiled by Jonathan Godfrey and Joseph Severn.

The author would like to thank the staff at the former National Gas Archive, Warrington, the National Monuments Record, the London Metropolitan Archives, Tower Hamlets Local History Library and Archives and the London Canal Museum for their help with the documentary research. Thanks are due to Liz Braby, curator of the Ragged School Museum, for her support and for arranging access to the museum. Kieron Tyler devised the research strategy for this publication. Ken Sabel provided valuable advice during the early stages of the project, while Michael Bussell contributed freely of his knowledge of engineering and industrial archaeology in his role as academic adviser to the publication project.

The images in Figs 3, 4, 7–11, 14–16, 18–21, 61–4 and 69–73 are reproduced with kind permission of Tower Hamlets Local History Library and Archives, and those in Figs 39, 51 and 58–9 with kind permission of the National Grid Archive (formerly National Gas Archive). Figs 13 and 53 are reproduced courtesy of Glendee (UK).

I stood with Mr Butler in the High Street of
Whitechapel amidst a blaze of light and amidst
the acclamation of the inhabitants. Our efforts
had not been in vain. From that moment our
Company was established.

James Holbert Wilson, of the Commercial Gas Light
and Coke Company, looking back on the early 1840s
(J Gas Sup, 11 April 1871, 279)

1

Introduction

1.1 Location and circumstances of the survey and research

This report presents the results of a building survey on the site of the former Commercial Gas Light and Coke Company's Stepney Gasworks, in the London Borough of Tower Hamlets. The site lay on the east side of Harford Street and west of the Regent's Canal (after 1929 known as the Grand Union Canal), and was some 3.37ha (8.33 acres) in extent. The Ordnance Survey National Grid reference for the centre of the site is 536270 181860 (Fig 1; Fig 2). The surveyed structures are placed in context through the results of extensive research into the history of the Company from its foundation in 1837 to the end of gas production at Stepney in 1945–6.

The Commercial Gas Light and Coke Company (contracted in the text to 'the Commercial Company' or 'the Company', to avoid confusion with its important rival, the Gas Light and Coke Company, also known as the Chartered Company) (Fig 3; Fig 4) was founded just as an 18-year-old Queen Victoria acceded to the throne, and finished its life as part of the gas industry nationalised by the Labour government of Clement Attlee. Its 112-year existence spanned the repeal of the Corn Laws, the Irish potato famine, the Great Stink, the *Origin of Species*, the rise of the Labour Party and trade unions, the development of railways, votes for women and the Boer, Crimean and First and Second World Wars. For a century east London's streets were lit with town gas made by the Commercial, as were its schools and sweatshops, its docks and synagogues, its police stations, brothels and churches. Later, gaslight found its way into working-class homes and gas was used for cooking and heating.

Since nationalisation, the name of the Commercial has gradually faded from memory, and its struggles with the Gas Light and Coke, the Great Central, the Ratcliff and other rival companies have been forgotten. The advent of natural gas in the 1960s rendered town gas obsolete, and gasworks that had been the physical expression in cement, brick and iron of Victorian confidence in progress and the future were largely dismantled.

By the end of the 20th century, there was not much left of the Commercial Company's works at Stepney. Most of the buildings had been demolished more than four decades earlier (Fig 5). The four surviving gasholders, adapted for natural gas storage, had gone out of use in the 1990s and the site had been earmarked for housing development. In a climate of increasing recognition of the importance of the industrial heritage generally, and that of the gas industry in particular (Trueman 1997; Tucker 2000), Museum of London Archaeology (MOLA, prior to 2009 known as the Museum of London Archaeology Service (MoLAS)) was commissioned to carry out an Industrial Heritage Assessment of the site (Tyler 1999) and in 2002 set about surveying the structures prior to demolition. Analytical surveys took place in November and December 2002, November and December 2004, and January 2005 (Tyler 2005). Both the surveys and the accompanying documentary

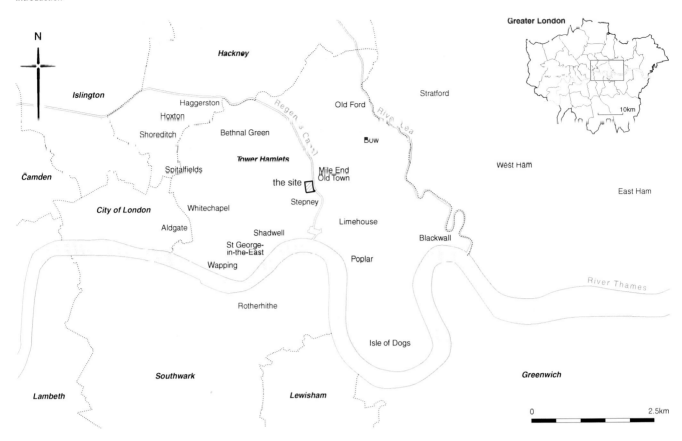

Fig 1 Location of the site and places mentioned in the text, showing adjacent London boroughs (italics) and their boundaries (dotted lines) (scale 1:75,000)

research were carried out as part of successive conditions on planning permission for redevelopment of the site by Bellway Homes.

The survey techniques employed by the MOLA team are more often used to record structures or earthworks of greater antiquity. The Victorian remains of the Stepney Works were photographed with 35mm and large-format film cameras, located with reference to the Ordnance Survey National Grid and recorded in plan and elevation to produce wire-frame computer representations. An elevated platform ('cherry-picker') was used to reach and record the higher parts of the gasholders that are usually inaccessible. The survey produced a broad and dimensionally accurate range of plans, elevations, sections and 3D drawings (Fig 6). The survey methodology is described in the method statements produced for the site (Tyler 2002, 2004).

Archaeology and history are not just about objects, but about people. Even the most detailed survey cannot on its own recreate the history of a site, which by the time of the MOLA survey was a skeletal remnant. The structures did not emerge fully formed from the ground, but were the result of an interplay of technological, social, political and economic forces; and a fuller understanding of the site can only be achieved by examining how these factors interconnected. As a result, the investigation was extended to recover the history of the Company and the people who worked for it.

As well as contemporary accounts, technical drawings, maps and photographs, one of the main documentary

sources was the Company's Minute Books. These large volumes record the meetings of the board in an almost continuous sequence, from 1844, seven years after the establishment of the Company, to nationalisation in 1949 and beyond (with one gap of about 20 months in the mid 1850s). Unfortunately it was not possible within the scope of this project to read each of the *c* 9400 pages of the Minute Books, but a good proportion was sampled, especially for the early formative years of the Company. For the latter part of the Company's history the Minute Books were indexed, which helped with the sampling process. An element of caution is needed in relying on the Minute Books as a source of history for the Company, since they often record only what the board intended to be done, rather than what was actually carried out (although of course if the board ordered something to be done, it is likely that the instruction was put into effect). By the same token, although it is often clear when actions were initiated, it is not so obvious when they were completed.

The late 19th century saw large-scale amalgamations of London's gas companies, especially into the Commercial's important neighbour, the Gas Light and Coke Company. Because of this, the history of the Gas Light and Coke Company (Everard 1949) encompasses not only that of other gas companies but most of the capital's gas industry too. However, it includes only passing mention of the Commercial, which refused to amalgamate with the Gas Light and Coke. As a result, the Company's history has not received the detailed attention it deserves. This book attempts to fill this gap in the story of London's gas industry, and is aimed at a wide readership – from residents of the London Borough of Tower Hamlets and those with a general interest in industrial history and archaeology, to specialists in the development of the gas industry and business history.

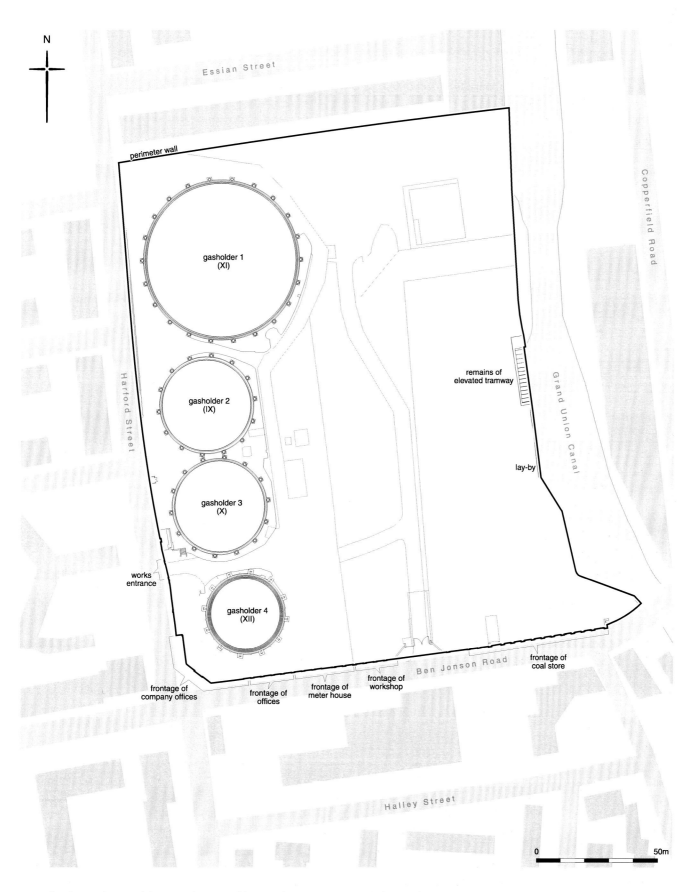

Fig 2 Plan showing the site and the principal remains of the gasworks surviving in 2003 (scale 1:1500)

*Fig 3 The Commercial Company's head office in 1931 (*Co-partnership H, *October 1935, 173)*

*Fig 4 The Stepney Works from the air in 1931, looking north-east (*Co-partnership H, *May 1931, 57)*

*Fig 5 The Stepney Works in 2003, looking north-west from the Grand Union Canal, showing (from left to right) gasholders 4 (**XII**), 3 (**X**), 2 (**IX**) and 1(**XI**)*

1.2 Organisation of this report

Because of the nature of the site and the extent of the historical evidence presented, this book is arranged slightly differently from other volumes in the MOLA Archaeology Studies Series. The report comprises six principal chapters. Chapter 2 sketches the 19th-century transformation of Victorian east London from a rural area at the edge of the metropolis to the cramped industrial district inhabited by the poor which it later became. This was the backdrop against which the Commercial Company developed. Chapter 3 explains how a typical Victorian gasworks functioned. The history of the Company in relation to the gas industry in London is explored in Chapter 4, while Chapter 5 charts how the Stepney Works itself developed, with the results of the MOLA building survey appearing in the relevant sections (Chapter 5.4–5.6). These chapters integrate evidence from the Minute Books with the MOLA survey results and other documentary and cartographic sources. The impact of the Company and the gas industry on the public and private domains is examined in Chapter 6, while Chapter 7 draws conclusions from these studies, and is followed by a bibliography of primary and secondary sources.

All paper, photographic and digital records, together with the full unpublished reports, have been deposited as the site archive. The archive is held under the site code HFD99 in the London Archaeological Archive and Research Centre (LAARC) at Mortimer Wheeler House, 46 Eagle Wharf Road, London N1 7ED, where it may be consulted by prior arrangement with the archive manager. Selected parts of the digital archive are also available.

1.3 Textual conventions

There were 12 gasholders overall in the history of the Stepney Gasworks, as one replaced another, and these were numbered in various ways during that time. To prevent confusion, for example between gasholder 1 in 1846 and the very different gasholder 1 50 years later, for the purposes of this book the gasholders are identified with the Roman numerals **I**–**XII**, with **I** being the earliest and **XII** the latest; these are given in square brackets in extracts from historic records which refer to the Company's own gasholder numbering. To identify other structures within the rapidly changing works, many of which are known only from documentary and cartographic sources, building numbers (B1–B21) are used in Chapter 5 and the reconstructions (see Fig 22).

Weights and measures quoted in the text are given where appropriate in the units used before metrication, with metric equivalents in brackets. One mile (1.61km) comprised 1760 yards, while a yard comprised 3 feet. A foot (0.30m) was divided into 12 inches (1in = 25.40µm). An acre is 0.4 hectare (ha); 1ha is about 2.5 acres. One ton (1016kg) comprised 20 hundredweight (1cwt = 50.8kg) or 2240 pounds, while one pound (0.45kg) comprised 16 ounces (1oz = 28g). One gallon equals about 4.55 litres (L). The measurements recorded during the building recording survey are given in metric units with imperial equivalents in brackets

In pre-decimal coinage there were 12 pence (d) to the shilling (s) and 20 shillings or 240d to the pound (£); 1s means one shilling (5p), and 2s 6d means two shillings and sixpence (12½p). A guinea was £1 1s 0d (£1.05).

During most of the period the Company was operating, gas was sold by the thousand cubic feet, often abbreviated to 'per thousand'. One thousand cubic feet is equal to 28.3m³. Coal and coke were measured in chaldrons, a rather elastic measure, one chaldron being equal to 36 bushels or between 1.25 and 1.31m³.

Gas pressure was measured in inches water gauge (1inH$_2$O at 4°C = 249.1N/m²). The quality of gas was generally measured in terms of its illuminating power, in 'candles'. The Metropolis Gas Act 1860 defined one candle in terms of the light produced by a pure sperm whale oil candle weighing one-sixth of a pound.

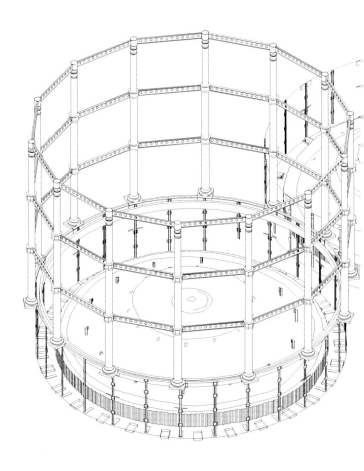

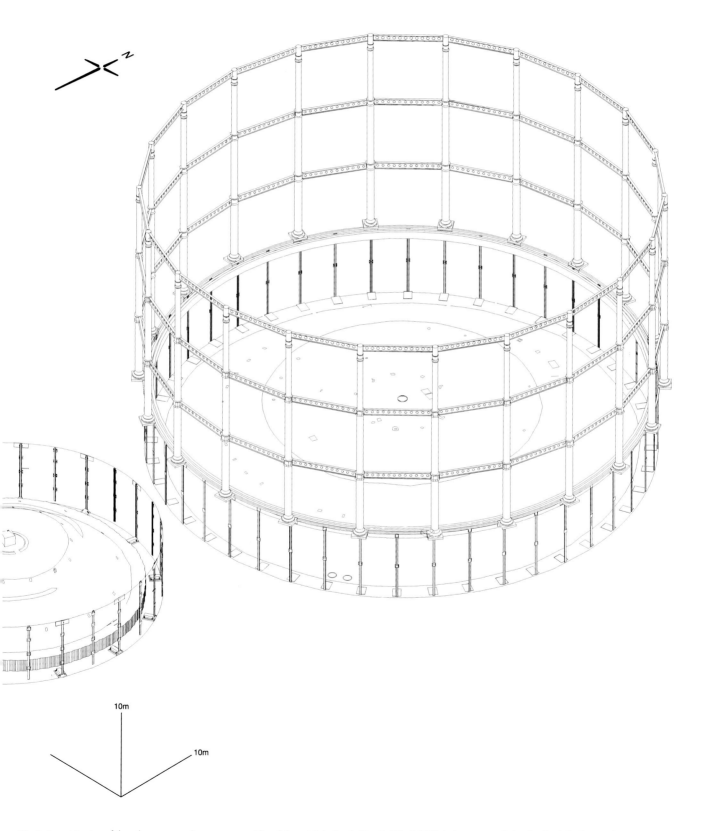

10m

10m

*Fig 6   Isometric view of the substructure and superstructure (from left to right) of gasholders 3 (**X**), 2 (**IX**) (substructure only) and 1 (**XI**) (scale 1:450)*

2

Victorian east London

2.1 Introduction

The phrase 'Victorian East End' conjures up images of docks, narrow streets and harsh poverty, contrasting with the riches of the City and the West End. However, this is only a partial picture. In the mid 19th century, when the Commercial Company was set up, the eastern side of the metropolis was an almost rural place, its centres of population having the character of distinct villages. It was only later in the century that east London became the home of the 'sweated labour' of shoe, furniture and clothing workers and a byword for poverty and suffering.

By the end of the 19th century Stepney was a district 'which industry and the poor can claim completely as their own' (*J Gas Sup*, 28 April 1908, 227). Industries in east London included jute manufacture, shipbuilding, paper staining, match manufacture, brewing and distilling, chemical works, soap and tallow manufacture, building, clothing manufacture, printing, the silk trade, gun making, animal and shell importing, India rubber manufacture, sail and rope making, candle making, leather goods manufacture, baking, and boot and shoe making as well as gas making (Glenny Crory 1876, 1).

2.2 Shipbuilding and the docks

In the first half of the 19th century, it was the old Port of London that gave the East End its character, spurring the development of shipbuilding and associated 'cottage' industries. Stevedores and lumpers who loaded and unloaded cargoes, ship repairers, ship's bakers, marine store dealers and watermen lived in a string of hamlets from the Tower to Limehouse, where the shipbuilding yards supported communities of skilled sailmakers and other craftsmen. There was also a seafaring tradition dating back hundreds of years, with accompanying public houses, disreputable lodging houses and brothels, especially along the Ratcliff Highway in Shadwell.

The villages of Poplar and Blackwall were built around the East India Company's main shipyards. The East India Company made its money importing tea, coffee, silks, spices and sugar from India, China, Japan and the East Indies, and local industries sprang up to handle the goods. A series of docks was constructed: the West India Dock on the Isle of Dogs in 1802 – big enough to accommodate 600 ships – the London Docks at Wapping, the East India Dock at Blackwall and the St Katharine Docks next to the Tower of London in 1828. The Commercial Road and the East India Dock Road were built to link these docks with the City.

In the second half of the 19th century, the need for larger docks to accommodate the steamships that replaced sail sparked a second wave of construction. The Royal Albert Dock, the West India South Dock and the Tilbury Docks sprang up.

These docks were a land-consuming duplication, forcing up land values to the ultimate detriment of the East End and its people (Ball and Sunderland 2001, 427). The immediate effect, however, was a change in the East End's character: street after street of poor quality terraces became home to tens of thousands of dockers and waterside workers. Immigrants, particularly from Ireland in the 1840s and 1850s, arrived for dock work, even though most of it was casual. By 1860 London's Irish population had risen to over 100,000, with many settling in the parishes of St George-in-the-East (located between Shadwell and Wapping), Stepney and Whitechapel (Weightman and Humphries 1983, 83).

London's shipbuilding industry fell into decline as iron replaced timber. London was a long way from the centres of coal and iron production, and many employers relocated to Tyneside and Clydeside. The industry's collapse meant that by 1867 there were 30,000 destitute in Poplar alone, with mechanics, shipbuilders and sailmakers reduced to taking casual work at the docks (Weightman and Humphries 1983, 87).

2.3　The rise of the sweatshop

As demand for mass-produced consumer goods increased in the second half of the 19th century, large wholesalers developed to supply an increasing number of retail outlets. The wholesalers broke down the work involved in the production of clothing and furniture – both major industries in the East End – into a large number of standardised tasks, each performed by a worker who did nothing but the assigned operation. The sweatshop system was designed to keep costs down to a minimum, and it was concentrated in Whitechapel, Bethnal Green and Stepney. Output and productivity were increased by exploiting cheap, unskilled labour in small overcrowded workshops or at home. This process was made more efficient in the middle of the century by the invention of simple, hand-driven machinery like the sewing machine, while the advent of gas lighting meant that longer hours could be worked.

A new geography of production was created, since the wholesaler needed to monitor subcontractors and home workers, and it was in the interests of these groups to be close to their employer. As a result, the production of consumer goods tended to be clustered in particular areas where low-paid, home-based workforces could afford to live. The workers employed in the new mass-market sectors were largely indigenous East End women and recent male immigrants. The women, poorly educated, were almost the entire workforce for dressmaking, and accounted for over 80% in shirt making, 40% in tailoring, and just under 10% in boot and shoe making. The immigrants were largely Jewish men, perhaps with knowledge of making clothes from their home country but restricted in their choice of employment by anti-Semitism, language and poor education. Entrepreneurial

and hardworking, many Jewish immigrants became masters themselves in the clothing industry (Ball and Sunderland 2001, 300–2).

'Slop' was the general term for clothing manufacture for independent wholesalers. Slop workers were generally located in Stepney and, to a lesser extent, Shoreditch and Bethnal Green. As the docks relocated, the trade shifted east to Bow and West Ham as the wives and daughters of the dockers migrated with the men (Ball and Sunderland 2001, 308). By 1861 the East End contained 34,000 tailors and tailoresses. The numbers increased most rapidly between 1881 and 1901, and by 1911 there were 65,000 (Schmiechen 1984, 38–9). Jobs included machinists, sewers, finishers, pressers, cutters, warehousemen and packers.

Silk weaving was also an East End industry in the early part of the Commercial's history; in 1838 there were 10,000 silk looms in the East End (Gibson 1958, 6) weaving raw silk that arrived from the Far East on East Indiamen. The skills had arrived with Huguenot refugees fleeing religious persecution in the late 17th century, but by the end of the 19th century the trade had collapsed.

Timber yards supplying the furniture making industry became established along the Regent's Canal. This industry produced poorer quality furniture goods than the bespoke makers based in the West End of London, and from 1860 moved east towards Bethnal Green and north to Hoxton (Ball and Sunderland 2001, 311).

2.4　The 'stink industries'

From the 1850s the 'stink industries', pushed out from other areas of the metropolis, capitalised on the pool of available labour in the East End, and established themselves in Stepney, Whitechapel, Bow and Old Ford. Glue was manufactured by boiling blood and bones. The production of matches, rubber, soap, tar and various other chemicals polluted the air and contaminated the water. Sulphuric acid vapour seeped out from the Rothschild family's mint near Whitechapel. With these industries came the poor, whose homes had been demolished elsewhere in the city to make way for new offices or later the railways, and who were forced to live in tenement 'doss houses' or terraced houses subdivided by rack-renting landlords.

Gas making itself can hardly be excluded from the definition of a stink industry. Although the use of gas was promoted as cleaner than coal in the early 19th century, the industry acquired a well-deserved reputation for filth. Gasworks generated smoke and dust from the furnaces as well as evil-smelling gases such as the rotten egg aroma of hydrogen sulphide. Noxious waste products such as ammoniacal liquor and blue billy (spent lime in water) were dumped in canals, in rivers or on waste ground, or found their way into the sewage system.

2.5 Increasing population

The population of the East End rose to dramatic heights in the latter half of the 19th century. Between 1841 and 1901, the numbers living in Bethnal Green increased from 74,000 to 130,000, in Poplar from 31,000 to 169,000 and in Stepney from 204,000 to 299,000 (Weightman and Humphries 1983, 90). The Commercial reaped the benefits of the increases in population, which supported the shops and public houses that were the Company's principal consumers in the first part of its history. Over 3000 shops and public houses were burning the Company's gas in 1847 (Maddocks 1931, 90). At the close of the 19th century, the invention of prepayment meters meant that the working class of east London could afford to light their homes with gas from the Stepney Works.

3

A Victorian gasworks

3.1 Introduction

This chapter describes the process of making gas in a typical 19th-century gasworks, but where information is available it specifically describes how gas was made at Stepney. At its simplest, the process of making coal gas at a gasworks can be briefly summarised. The gas is produced by the destructive distillation of coal, which is heated at about 600–1000°C in the absence of air in closed cylinders known as retorts. The gas that is driven off is purified, stored in gasholders and delivered to the mains. Such coal gas contained about 40% methane, 40% hydrogen and 10% carbon dioxide, with other hydrocarbons, carbon monoxide and nitrogen making up the remaining 10%. The by-products include coke (from the coal), tar and ammonium sulphate. Fig 7, although depicting the plant in use in the 1930s Stepney Works, illustrates the main stages required for any industrial scale production.

The heat treatment of coal in this way is called carbonisation, and the resulting gas is known as coal gas. Combustible gas can also be produced using other, similar methods, for example by heating brown coal, coke and oil – known as gasification (Stewart 1958, 1). Town gas is the generic name given to any combination of combustible gases distributed from localised sources of production via underground pipes to the premises of domestic, commercial and industrial users (ibid).

3.2 Raw materials

Ease of delivery of raw materials was essential for gasworks. Most London gasworks were located near canals or with river access, and later near railways, to facilitate the delivery of coal. At Stepney in the 1860s, the coals were worked out of barges by eight men acting as a counterbalance to the coal basket (Maddocks 1931, 222). Later, cranes and a coal tramway were installed. Coking coal generally came from Newcastle, Durham and Yorkshire, and the richer cannel coal from Scotland and Lancashire.

The coal was best kept under cover, since wet coal reduced gas yield, so it was kept in a coal store prior to use. It was usual practice to hold about two weeks' consumption at a works, and a ton of coal occupied some 40 to 48 cubic feet (1.13 to 1.36m³) (Clegg 1853, 172). The stacks of coal were retained by 3in (80mm) planks, placed vertically and strutted (ibid). Tie plates were used in the walls of coal stores to withstand lateral pressure from the stacked coal. Ventilation was essential to prevent the build-up of inflammable gases.

Coke was also stored before sale. Later works incorporated coal and coke handling plants. Other raw materials and by-products that needed storage were lime and – from about the 1850s – iron oxide for use in purification, and spent and waste lime.

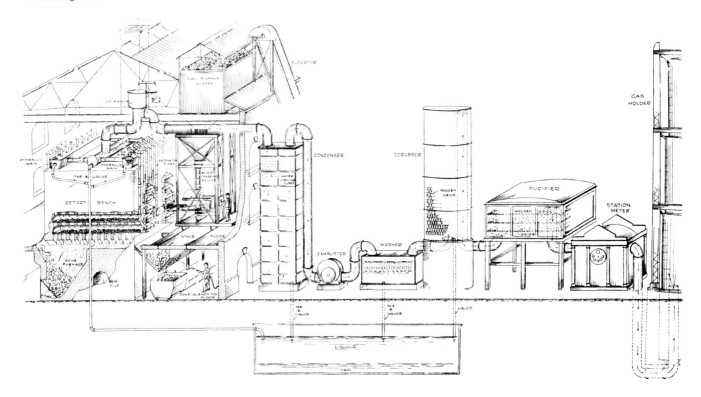

Fig 7 The manufacture of coal gas in the 1930s at the Stepney Works (Co-partnership H, May 1931, 69)

3.3   The retort house

The retort house was the heart of a gasworks. After the coal had been crushed into pieces no more than 1in (25.4mm) diameter it was loaded into closed cylinders, usually with a D-shaped section (with the flat side downwards), known as retorts (Fig 8). The retorts were heated directly from a furnace burning coal or (later) coke, produced from earlier gas making. One authority in 1848 reported that London gasworks used coke and tar for the furnaces (Taylor 1848, 7). Several retorts heated by the same furnace were known as an oven, and a row of adjoining ovens was known as a retort bench. An oven consisted of a group of five or so retorts arranged around a furnace and set within a brick arch. A large retort house might contain 20 or so such arches with a capacity of 45 tons of coal daily (Stewart 1958, 12). Horizontal retorts became the standard and, with successive improvements, remained the sole means of carbonisation in the gas industry until about 1890 (ibid, 12–13). They were adaptable to a wide range of coals and relatively simple to operate. Although variations such as the vertical retort were developed early in the 19th century, even in the late 1950s horizontal retorts accounted for a quarter of the carbonising capacity of the gas industry (ibid). The larger 7ft (2.13m) long retorts could hold $2^{1}/_{2}$ cwt (127kg) of coal that could be carbonised in six hours (ibid, 12).

Low temperature carbonisation was carried out at about 600°C, and high temperature at about 1000°C. The fireman judged the temperature of the retorts through sight holes in the brickwork or by the appearance of the retorts when opened. Iron retorts were kept 'cherry red', and clay retorts – which could withstand a higher temperature – 'between a cherry red and a bright orange' (Colburn 1865, 28).

The gas, mixed with impurities, was driven off as a yellow-brown smoke with a temperature of about 80°C. This was removed via ascension pipes, passing through a non-return liquid seal in a large closed trough half-filled with water called a hydraulic main (Trueman 1997, 10). At Stepney, the hydraulic main was wrought iron (Colburn 1865, 31). The hydraulic main collected hot tar and ammonia which dissolved in the water and was continuously drawn off through a tar tower (Fig 9) and into a liquor tank and tar well. Meanwhile, the gas passed through the foul main, a large pipe which cooled the gas and took it to the purifiers (Trueman 1997, 10).

In high temperature carbonisation, one ton of average coal yielded 14,000 cubic feet ($400m^3$) of gas, with by-products of 10cwt (508kg) of coke, 10 gallons (45.5L) of tar, 3 to 4 gallons (13.7–18.2L) of benzole (if extracted), 10 pounds (4.5kg) of sulphur and 28 pounds (12.7kg) of ammonia (as sulphate) (Stewart 1958, 2). In low temperature carbonisation, one ton of coal yielded 4500 cubic feet ($127.43m^3$) of gas equalling 42 therms (or *c* 1230.6 kilowatt hours of electrical energy), *c* 20 gallons (91L) of tar and an easily ignitable coke (ibid).

When carbonised, coking coals produced good quality coke and gas which burned at *c* 5 cubic feet ($0.14m^3$) per hour in an Argand burner (Chapter 6.2), yielding a light of 12 to 18 candles. Only a poor coke was produced from the more expensive cannel coal, but a richer gas of 20 to 28 candles (Stewart 1958, 18). The Commercial was using predominantly coking coal, but from the 1850s mixed its gas with gas produced from cannel coal to improve illuminating power. The Company's use of cannel coal increased from the 1860s into the

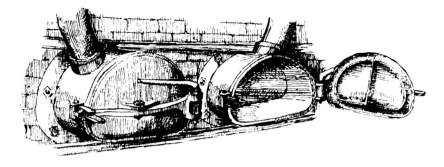

Fig 8 Two horizontal retorts, one with the mouthpiece open and one closed
(Co-partnership H, September 1932, 166)

Fig 9 A tar tower
(Co-partnership H,
October 1932, 178)

early 1870s as successive pieces of legislation stipulated a minimum illuminating power. Other companies sold gas made only from cannel coal and distributed it in separate mains from gas made from coking coal. By 1873, improvements in burners had lessened the need for cannel gas, and it was rendered obsolete by enrichment of coal gas with naphthalene or benzole vapours and finally by carburetted water gas (see below) that could be produced at short notice with an illuminating power of 14 to 30 candles (Stewart 1958, 19).

In the early years of the industry, retorts were made from iron, but later these were superseded by clay retorts. The advantages of iron retorts were that they were good conductors of heat and non-porous. However, in contact with coal or coke they absorbed carbon and expanded. A 7ft (2.13m) retort would lengthen to 7ft 6in (2.29m), disturbing the brickwork setting. Iron retorts were also damaged by high temperature and could not be repaired; their useful life was generally 200 days (Stewart 1958, 13). The Stepney Works was reconstructed from the early 1850s when the Company switched to the predominant use of retorts made from moulded fireclay, universally referred to as 'clay retorts', and generally adopted after 1853 (ibid). They had a life of 600 to 1000 days, could be repaired, suffered from less distortion than iron, and could be used at higher temperatures – 1000°C to 1100°C. However, their porous nature meant that to avoid leakage gas had to be removed at low pressure by means of pumps known as exhausters; and they also increased fuel consumption.

The iron lids of the retorts were closed by a screw clip, and then sealed with clay. The self-sealing retort lid was introduced in 1869 by Robert Morton (Stewart 1958, 14). These lids were the entry point for the coal at the beginning of the process, and were also used to discharge coke at the end. The earliest retorts were charged with coal by shovel, the coke being removed by rake. As retorts became longer, the 'throw' of the shovel became more difficult and scoop-charging was introduced. The U-shaped, 9ft (2.74m) long scoop was operated by a 'scoop gang' of three men. Mechanisation followed by 1910, using projector and 'shot' types of machine (ibid).

Carburetted water gas (CWG) plant was installed at Stepney at the end of the 19th century to supplement the retort houses. CWG plant allowed large volumes of gas to be generated in a short space of time. The production of carburetted water gas consisted of a combination of two methods: passing steam

through white-hot coke, thus forming a gas containing equal amounts of carbon monoxide and hydrogen; and cracking gas oil or other hydrocarbon oils in contact with hot brickwork (Stewart 1958, 20). Carburetted water gas and oil gases underwent the same purification process as coal gas, apart from the removal of ammonia, which they did not contain (ibid, 29).

3.4 Purification

The next stage in gas making was purification. Tar had to be removed, as well as impurities that did not aid the lighting process, such as carbon dioxide, oxygen and nitrogen, and gases that produced an unpleasant effect when burnt, such as ammonia, hydrogen sulphide and sulphur compounds. Badly purified gas had an adverse effect on trade since it caused respiratory complaints as well as attacking gilding, jewellers' goods and leather – for example in shoe shops (Taylor 1848, 6).

Early purification consisted of washing the gas in a suspension of slaked lime. Such 'wet' lime washers were used until the mid 1840s, but a major disadvantage was the large amount of spent lime in water (blue billy) produced. At the Gas Light and Coke Company's Westminster Works in the 1810s, this evil-smelling liquid was initially stored in large, leaking tanks after the company was refused use of the sewers. Eventually, the Gas Light and Coke agreed to pay the river authorities an annual 'fine' for discharging the effluent directly into the river (Everard 1949, 65).

Later developments involved a four-stage purification process (Fig 7). First, condensers (a long run of piping cooled by air or water) condensed out tar and ammonia (Fig 10). Vertical condensers used a water jet to precipitate out the tar. The multiple inverted U-tube air-cooled condenser was designed in 1817 (Trueman 1997, 14). The next two stages – washing and scrubbing – used water to absorb more tar and ammonia. In washers, devised in 1817, gas passed through perforated wooden boards running with water. The design was improved in the late 1860s and early 1870s. The tower scrubber was devised by George Lowe in 1846 (Stewart 1958, 24) to remove the remaining ammonia by spraying the gas from the top of the tower with water as it passed over shelving. There was a great variation of condensers across London. Some engineers insisted on 5 square feet ($1.53m^2$) of surface for every 1000 cubic feet ($28.32m^3$) of gas produced in 24 hours, but others managed with less (Colburn 1865, 33).

The final stage was purification. 'Dry' lime washers were devised in 1817 (Trueman 1997, 15), but used extensively from the 1860s (Fig 11). They avoided the production of blue billy effluent by passing the gas over slats holding damp burnt lime. There were experiments in using various metal oxides in the 1840s, and by 1853 iron oxide, especially with 'revivication' which restored its properties, was generally used for purification (Stewart 1958, 24). The iron oxide removed hydrogen sulphide compounds, while lime removed sulphur compounds. The

Fig 10 An atmospheric condenser (Co-partnership H, July 1932, 103)

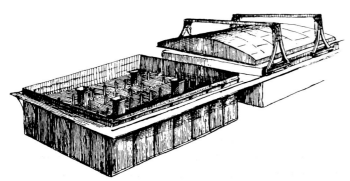

Fig 11 A gas purifier (Co-partnership H, August 1932, 125)

purifiers consisted of large cast iron boxes containing trays of dry lime or iron oxide, with piping and valves to control the cycle of use of the boxes (Trueman 1997, 15).

3.5 Gasholders

Gasholders – half building, half machine (Tucker 2000, 6) – were the most visible components of a gasworks. Many still dominate the urban skyline.

Gas companies considered it desirable to have a storage capacity at least equal to the maximum daily production of their gasworks to avoid the risk of running out of gas (Tucker 2000, 34); so as demand spurred greater production, gasholders increased in size. The storage vessel in a gasholder, known as a bell, is a light but rigid container – originally of wrought iron, later of steel – closed at the top and sides, but open at the bottom, which is partially immersed in a tank of water acting as a seal. A guide frame prevents the bell from tipping over and allows it to move freely up and down (ibid, 36). When full, the bell rises almost out of the tank. The slightly domed roof of the bell is called the crown, and its top and bottom edges the top curb and bottom curb.

In larger holders, the sides of the bell are made telescopic in two or more lifts, with a water seal between each pair of lifts. The lifts are concentric cylinders, nested within each other (Tucker 2000, 36). The lifts of telescopic gasholders are invariably sealed by a cup-and-grip water seal. The cup is an annular trough, riveted around the bottom edge of the upper (inner) lift, while a similar but inverted and reversed form, the grip, is fixed inside the top of the lower (outer) lift, hooking into the cup. As the upper lift rises out of the tank, the cup picks up both the lower lift and a quantity of water, which provides the seal (ibid, 38).

The guide rails of column-guided gasholders are engaged by rollers mounted at the top and bottom of the bell and the tops of the individual lifts in telescopic gasholders. Further internal rollers hold one lift against the next. The brackets supporting the rollers are known as carriages (Tucker 2000, 41) (Fig 12).

The form of construction of the crown of a gasholder was a major aspect of its design (Tucker 2000, 62). Untrussed crowns, reliant entirely on external support from below when in the unpressurised state, were introduced about 1850 (ibid, 63). When 'grounded', untrussed crowns were supported on a rest frame of timber or sometimes iron, which was built up from the bottom of the tank (Fig 13). It was essential to make the top curb very robust, and this was usually achieved with two or more heavy angle irons joined by thick plates, often making a U or box section (ibid, 62–3).

The water tank of a gasholder was a major engineering feat, since it had to hold some 500–700 gallons (2273–3182L) of water for each 100 cubic feet ($2.83m^3$) of inner bell capacity (Stewart 1958, 34). Construction of these water tanks was a specialist undertaking, and the depths of excavation exceeded

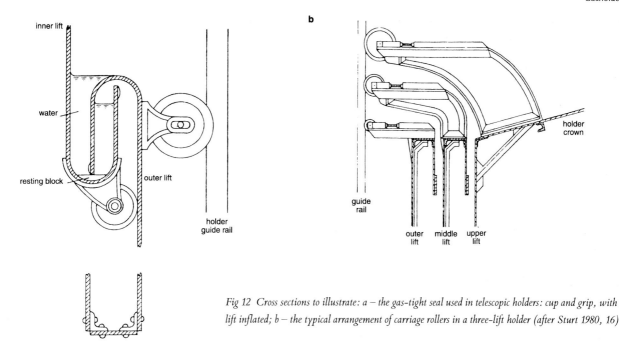

a
inner lift
water
resting block
outer lift
holder guide rail

b
holder crown
guide rail
outer lift middle lift upper lift

Fig 12 Cross sections to illustrate: a – the gas-tight seal used in telescopic holders: cup and grip, with lift inflated; b – the typical arrangement of carriage rollers in a three-lift holder (after Sturt 1980, 16)

*Fig 13 The timber rest frame structure of gasholder 2 (**IX**) during demolition, looking south (Glendee 2004, photograph 14)*

those of docks and early sub-surface railways (Tucker 2000, 70).

A flat-topped cone of earth in the centre of the tank is known as the 'dumpling'. The dumpling reduces the volume of excavation and has a counterbalance effect on the forces of the ground (Tucker 2000, 69). If the bell has an untrussed crown, a rest frame of wooden or iron posts and cross-members is built up from the dumpling; otherwise there is usually a central rest pillar of brickwork or similar (ibid).

Below-ground tanks were principally built of brick for much of the 19th century (Tucker 2000, 68). The brick walls were backed with a sealing layer of puddle clay (ibid, 69) to prevent water leaking into the ground, a technique commonly used in canal and dock building. Puddle clay was clay wetted to a plastic consistency and compacted in layers to a solid waterproof mass (ibid, 71). The underlying London Clay provided a naturally waterproof base for the gasholders at Stepney.

The bottom of the tank, including the dumpling, was often protected by 6in (15mm) or more of concrete, although this was not feasible before Portland cement became widely available in the 1860s; paving slabs could also be used (Tucker 2000, 69). At the Stepney Works the tanks were usually filled with water from the canal, to a level which would have been within a few inches of the top of the coping (ibid). Gas was admitted and expelled through pipes rising inside the tank which might be controlled by external valves (ibid, 36).

In water-sealed gasholders, the weight of the bell was supported and balanced by the upward pressure of the gas upon the crown, so the weight determined the pressure in the holder (Tucker 2000, 38). Gasholders were designed to 'throw' a pressure at least equal to what was considered necessary to drive the gas through the district mains and maintain a minimum pressure to the consumer. Variations in pressure were controlled by a station governor (ibid).

3.6 Pumps, station meters and governors

Exhausters were pumps that assisted the passage of gas through the various parts of the plant in the gasworks (Tucker 2000, 38), as well as providing the energy to lift the bells of the gasholders, which in turn pressurised the mains (Stewart 1958, 34–5) (Fig 14). Exhausters were initially driven by steam engine and later by gas engine, steam turbine or electric pump (Trueman 1997, 16). These components could be housed in an engine house.

Station meters were specialised pieces of equipment that measured the quantity of gas manufactured. In London, these were almost always made by Crosley or Parkinson (Colburn 1865, 66); the latter constructed station meters for the Stepney Works in 1848, 1853 and 1865.

The station governor maintained a constant predetermined pressure of gas leaving the works and entering the mains (Fig 15). Initial pressure at the gasholders depended on construction and the number of lifts engaged, since the weight of the bell provided the pressure, but it was normally 3 to 12inH$_2$O (750–3100N/m^2). At the station governor, the pressure was controlled to between 3 and 7inH$_2$O (750–1700N/m^2). At the consumer's premises the pressure was between about 2.5 and 4inH$_2$O (620–1000N/m^2) (Stewart 1958, 37).

3.7 Mains

In the early days of the industry, mains laying followed routes already settled by water distribution. The gas mains pipes were almost entirely cast iron, and joined either by flange joints or cast lead filled sockets. The turned and bored socket and spigot joint was developed in 1826, and this and the cast lead filled sockets remained the standard joints for 100 years (Stewart 1958, 39). The pipes were cast in pit moulds; only from 1919 was the superior spun cast method used (ibid).

The mains were low pressure, with the main proceeding through the principal avenue of an area; pressure was maintained by decreasing the diameter of the pipe as the distance from the gasworks increased. Branches were taken to each street from the main, and service pipes connected the branches to consumers. From the meter, a series of pipes buried in the walls and floor of the building proceeded to the supply cocks of individual appliances. The pipe system in a building was known as 'carcassing'.

In the 1810s gun barrels from the Napoleonic wars were converted into service pipes, and cannons were occasionally used for lamp-posts – an industrial variant of 'swords into ploughshares'. The word 'barrel' was still employed by the gas industry well into the 20th century to describe small diameter pipes (Everard 1949, 68).

3.8 The work

There were many jobs at a gasworks, from blacksmiths to clerks, from storekeepers to yard labourers, but most of the men toiled in the retort houses, and it was this work that characterised a gasworks. A gasworks with 300 long retorts would provide employment for 300 men, half on the day shift and half working at night (Colburn 1865, 25) (Fig 16).

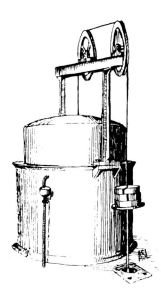

Fig 15 A gas governor (Co-partnership H, *April 1932, 40*)

Fig 14 A gas exhauster (Co-partnership H, *June 1932, 80*)

The men were usually divided into gangs of five – three carbonisers or stokers to work the retorts, a fourth man to keep up the fires in the furnaces and a fifth to barrow the coal and coke. The gang worked 42–56 mouthpieces (one retort with openings at each end comprising two mouthpieces) every 12-hour shift, for seven days a week, with the exception of one, sometimes two, Sundays a month. When the mouthpieces were not in the same range of benches, the men would have to go from one retort house to the next to complete their shift. The severest work was drawing or raking out the retorts, although at least 45 minutes were allowed for the work of charging and drawing that might only take 15–20 minutes (ibid, 24).

At many London works, the men were provided with an unlimited supply of a water and oatmeal mix or 'skilly' – at the Gas Light and Coke's Westminster Works each stoker consumed 7 quarts (6.6 litres) of this a day. One man there, who incautiously drank cold water instead while overheated, 'dropped dead to the ground' (Colburn 1865, 24–5).

Demand for gas varied with the time of day, the day and the season. In spring and summer, demand could drop to almost a quarter of that for winter. Men were laid off, a large proportion of them seeking employment in brickmaking, and returning to the gasworks in the autumn (Colburn 1865, 25). Those who toiled at the Stepney Works were 'a rough class of men, strong, ignorant and illiterate, many of whom were married, with large families, living in over-crowded lodgings of the poorest description' (Maddocks 1931, 222).

The working conditions were hard. The description by a French visitor, Flora Tristan, of what she saw at the Westminster Works in the 1830s, vividly conveys the sights and smells of a gasworks: 'Everything is made of iron – platform, railings, staircases, floors, roofing etc – plainly no expense has been spared to ensure that buildings and equipment alike are made of the most durable materials' (Tristan 1982, 72). Inside the retort house, when the spent coke was raked out, fire 'thrust out' from the retorts and the coke 'fell in blazing torrents … the cavern [was] suddenly illuminated with living fire, descending like a waterfall from a rocky height' (ibid, 74). The incandescent coke, much enlarged from the original size of the coal and cohering in a single mass, had to be broken up by the men with long-handled rakes (Colburn 1865, 29). As the coke was quenched with water 'there arose a dense hot whirlwind of black smoke that ascended majestically through the open skylight' (Tristan 1982, 74). There was no escape outside the retort house: 'the air is horribly tainted, at every instant you are assailed by poisonous fumes … everywhere I went, the foul exhalations of gas and the stench of coal and tar pursued me' (ibid, 73).

Her shock, however, was reserved for the condition of the 'sullen, silent and impassive' men, in 'nothing but cotton

Fig 16 A scoop charging gang at Stepney in 1897 – left to right: W Stamborough (who left the Company's service owing to ill health in 1924), R G Knight (who became a retort house foreman and was pensioned in 1930), E Jones (who became a night watchman and was pensioned in 1923) and E Tuckwell (who left the Company soon after the photo was taken in 1897) (Co-partnership H, March 1932, 22)

drawers' (Tristan 1982, 73), simply throwing a coat over their shoulders after the work was done.

There were about twenty men present, going about their work in a slow, deliberate fashion. Those with nothing to do stood motionless, lacking the energy even to wipe away the sweat streaming down their bodies … The foreman told me that only the strongest men were selected as stokers; even so, they all developed chest diseases after seven or eight years of work, and invariably died of consumption. (Ibid, 72–3)

Another observer, who visited the Stepney Works in the late 19th century, said that although the work 'is exacting, it is not slavish', conceding, however, that 'a person who indulged in turtle soup, crusted port or alcohol in any shape would make a poor retort man' (Glenny Crory 1876, 40).

4

The Commercial Company

4.1 The beginnings of the gas industry

The Commercial Company was set up in 1837, some 25 years after the establishment in London of the world's first gas company. However, the roots of the discovery and manufacture of gas reach back much further. The existence of 'inflammable airs' had been noted in the late 16th century and by the 17th and 18th centuries there was systematic investigation and experimentation into gas manufacture. Notable milestones include the Revd John Clayton announcing to the Royal Society in 1688 that gas could be extracted from a fuel and used for light; James Spedding collecting mine gas to light a works office at Whitehaven colliery in Cumberland in 1765; Lord Dundonald (Archibald Cochrane) lighting parts of his house at Culross Abbey, Perthshire, in 1782, with gas derived from a process that extracted tar and pitch from coal; and William Murdock lighting his office in Redruth, Cornwall, in 1792 with gas from coal carbonised in a retort. By the end of the 18th century, a reasonable understanding of the chemistry of gas manufacture was in place and this, combined with the demand for artificial lighting, marks the birth of the gas industry (Trueman 1997, 22). Murdock, a gas industry pioneer, went on to build an experimental gas plant to light Boulton and Watt's Soho foundry in Birmingham in 1802.

The process of carbonising coal to produce coke became well established after Abraham Darby developed the coke smelting of iron in 1709, but the gas produced was initially considered a waste product and piped away (Trueman 1997, 22). Increasingly, however, the importance of gas was recognised, and technological advances drove developments in gas lighting. In 1782 Lavoisier devised the forerunner of the gasholder: a cubical wooden framework covered with sheet iron, with the bottom end open and submerged in water (ibid, 16). Inspired by Dundonald's work, Murdock recognised the commercial advantages of gas and made its production, rather than that of coke, tar and pitch, the focus of his experiments in the last years of the 18th century (Everard 1949, 14).

As the Industrial Revolution gathered pace, the artificial light supplied by oil lamps or tallow and wax candles could no longer meet the needs of industry. One experimenter, Friedrich Accum, claimed in the late 1800s that the light of a single gas lamp was equal to that of three tallow candles or 18 oil lamps (Everard 1949, 23). In 1813 it was estimated that the cost of candles would have been two-and-a-half times more than the cost of the gas used (ibid, 35). Safety was also a factor: the snuffing out of candles caused sparks which, particularly in textile factories, could lead to devastating fires. Significantly, it was this industry that benefited first from gaslight, with the Phillips and Lee cotton mill in Salford and Henry Lodge's cotton mill at Sowerby Bridge installing systems in 1805–6 (Giles and Goodall 1992, 60; Trueman 1997, 23–4).

Dundonald, Murdock and others were convinced that gaslight was best suited to factories, rather than private homes (Everard 1949, 20–1). It was a German entrepreneur, Friedrich Winzer (soon anglicised to Frederic Winsor), who arrived in

England in 1803, who recognised the benefits of a 'central station' system, in which a central gasworks delivered gas to consumers via street mains in the same way as water. Winsor was a determined proselytiser for gas and praised its benefits, sometimes in outrageous terms: for example, he asserted that a £50 share in a gas company would yield an annual interest of £6000 (ibid, 19), a claim that would have surprised even a shareholder in the South Sea Company. He had, however, developed the methods used by Philippe Lebon to light Paris with gas, which attracted backers and led to the founding of the first gas company. The Gas Light and Coke Company fought opposition to obtain its royal charter in 1812; it was also known as the Chartered Company, although it reverted to the former name from the late 19th century onwards (ibid, 250).

London was the ideal place for such a venture. The metropolis was rapidly expanding; there was a large, wealthy market; and coal was relatively cheap compared with other lighting fuels such as oil and tallow (Trueman 1997, 25). It was a city of narrow streets, courts and alleyways, full of dark corners which at night provided hiding places for petty thieves and pickpockets. It was policed by watchmen (the Metropolitan Police was not established until 1829), and well-to-do pedestrians relied on 'link boys' with flaming torches to light their path. The street light afforded by oil lamps was 'dismal' (quoted in Stewart 1958, 43).

The Gas Light and Coke Company erected the first permanent gasworks for public supply in Westminster (Everard 1949, 38) and the company's financial success made it a model for others as the industry grew. By 1820 15 towns in England and Scotland had gas undertakings; this number had increased to 200 such towns a decade later and at least 760 by 1849 (Trueman 1997, 25–6).

Despite the difficulties, the gas industry expanded rapidly. In London by 1817 there were 20 miles (32km) of street mains, but six years later there were 215 miles (346km; Clegg 1853, 22). In 1824 the capital's entire gas industry used 50,000 tons of coal (ibid); under 30 years later the same quantity was consumed by the Commercial's Stepney Works alone (LMA, B/CGC/3, 235 (13 May 1853)). With increasing competition, improvements in technology and pressure from legislation the price of gas fell – from 15s per thousand cubic feet in 1817 to 4s 6d per thousand in 1851 (Clegg 1853, 22).

Many gas companies were established by individual Acts of Parliament authorising the building of works and the breaking up of streets to lay mains, and specifying gas quality and level of shareholders' dividends. Companies without such statutory powers operated at a disadvantage, since they had to obtain permission from parish authorities to lay mains.

The relations between the gas companies themselves were always fractious, seesawing from painstaking boundary negotiations to attempts to drive one another out of business. Government intervention further complicated this relationship. In the early years of the industry, successive Tory governments promoted the idea of regulated monopoly to benefit consumers, even imposing exclusive districts of supply on

companies (Everard 1949, 96). In 1830 this policy was turned on its head by the new Liberal government, which believed in unrestrained competition (ibid, 92). Although the change in policy pushed the price of gas down to more affordable levels (ibid, 134), it was accompanied by an intense and sometimes corrupt rivalry. In the 1830s companies hired canvassers, known as 'foot-in-the-door men', who cajoled, misled or intimidated consumers into taking their gas. Consumers were presented with bills from companies that did not supply them. Gangs of mains layers disturbed pipes belonging to competitors, despite the risk of explosion, and services were connected up to the mains of rival companies. Companies reduced gas quality, slashed wages and neglected maintenance in order to cut costs and offer huge discounts to consumers which their competitors could not match (ibid, 101–3). This was the environment into which the Commercial Company was born (Fig 17).

4.2 Fighting for survival, 1837–44

The proposal for the Commercial Company was first put forward in 1836 by Charles Hunt of Stepney (Maddocks 1931, 22) who envisaged it being run by consumers themselves. He was among many dissatisfied with the quantity, quality and price of gas supplied to the area east of the metropolis by the competing Gas Light and Coke, British, Ratcliff, and Poplar companies. The idea was that a company controlled by its consumers would supply good quality gas at a reasonable price, and that the money saved would be reinvested in the company. The Commercial Company thus started life in 1837 as an association of consumers.

James Goldie and John Lamont, respectively a distiller and a brewer (LBTH, L/SGE/J/4/30, resolution of 22 October 1840), became involved, along with others with influence in Whitechapel and Bethnal Green. A canvass of prospective consumers was organised which showed that an annual income of £11,000 could be expected (Maddocks 1931, 23). The consumers were asked to form a committee of 'proprietors' to finance and promote the Company. A significant proportion of the consumers were shopkeepers, reflecting the fact that in this period the supply of gas to light private homes was too expensive for most, and many were licensed victuallers, which led to the Company becoming nicknamed 'The Licensed Victuallers' Company' (ibid).

The site selected for the Commercial's works was open land to the east of the main part of Stepney, which clustered around Stepney Green and St Dunstan's Church. Maps of 1746 and 1827 show this part of Ben Jonson Fields as undeveloped (Rocque 1746; Greenwood and Greenwood 1827 (below, Fig 23)). A nearby road was even called 'World's End'. By the second decade of the 19th century, the fields and orchards were being converted into house plots and industries were becoming established – particularly ropewalks, which

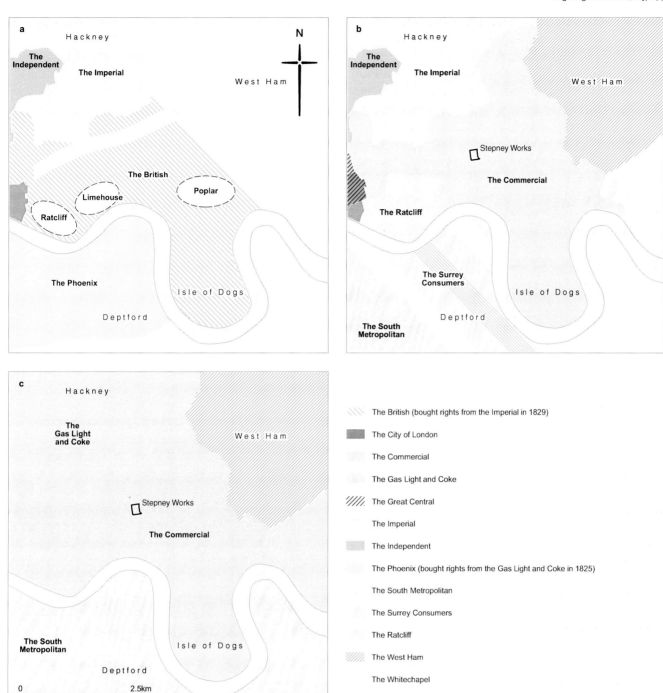

Fig 17 Gas companies supplying east London in: a – 1820s; b – 1860; c – 1880 (after Everard 1949, opposite pages 96, 192, 240) (scale 1:80,000)

served Thames-side shipyards to the south. A major factor in the selection of Stepney as an ideal site for a gasworks was the presence of the Regent's Canal, which opened in 1820. The canal was the first in London to allow colliers to use it, and the coal trade from north-east England developed quickly, particularly after its dock was enlarged in the 1830s and 1840s.

The Company was constituted on 15 February 1839 as a joint stock company formed by deed of settlement. A clause limited the liability of subscribers to the number of shares they held. A prospectus was prepared and the public offer of the

shares attracted 350 signatures, overwhelmingly from consumers. Twenty thousand shares at £5 each were issued, giving the Company a nominal capital of £100,000. Only a deposit had to be paid on each share but the subscribed capital was enough to build retort and purifying houses with a tank on 4½ acres (1.8ha) of land leased in December 1837 at Ben Jonson Fields, and to construct a lay-by on the Regent's Canal (Maddocks 1931, 24). Offices in the City of London were established at 60 King William Street; James Goldie was appointed chairman and John Lamont deputy chairman. The directors were Charles Salisbury Butler, James Holbert Wilson,

George Wildbore, L C Lescesne and B J Hedges, with Griffith Thomas the company solicitor (ibid). Charles Hunt had left the Company after a disagreement (ibid, 23).

The directors and a committee of 14 proprietors managed the Company, with each director holding at least 60 shares and a member of the committee 20 shares. Monthly meetings of shareholders were organised, and the voting strengths at general meetings were set to favour the smaller investor, with 1 vote for 2 shares, 2 votes for 5 shares, 3 votes for 20 shares, 4 votes for 40 shares and 5 votes for 60 or more shares (Maddocks 1931, 24).

Rival companies looked on in alarm. The Gas Light and Coke Company supplied Spitalfields and Bethnal Green in east London, although its main area of supply was the City. Its east London works was located in Brick Lane. The Gas Light and Coke had failed to capitalise on the demand for gas in east London principally because of a shortage of holders and poor gas pressure (Everard 1949, 82–3), allowing rival gas companies to flourish. One of these was the British Gas Light Company, incorporated in 1829, which had works in Schoolhouse Lane, Ratcliff, and in Old Ford Road near Bow Church. It supplied West Ham, Bow and Limehouse, and shared the supply of Ratcliff, Mile End Old Town and Whitechapel with the Ratcliff Company. The Ratcliff Company, incorporated in 1823, also supplied Aldgate, Shadwell, and parts of Wapping and St George's. It had purchased the East London Gas Light and Coke Company, and had recently moved its works from Sun Tavern Fields (Cable Street) to New Crane, Wapping. The Poplar Company, incorporated in 1821, supplied Poplar and other places adjacent to the parish from its works in Back Lane, Poplar. The Imperial Company had bought the gasworks at Limehouse in 1824 (ibid, 159).

The Commercial first turned its attention to the supply of Wapping, Shadwell and St George's parishes. The Ratcliff Company reacted by using its strong family and business connections to frustrate the Commercial's efforts. Despite the Commercial marshalling the support of consumers in the area, the Commissioners of Ratcliff Pavement and the Trustees of the Commercial Road not only refused the Commercial permission to lay mains (NGA, NT, COG/A/C/1, 3 December 1841), but passed resolutions to the effect that they were satisfied with the existing public lighting and that a new company was not required (Maddocks 1931, 38).

Surviving documents from 1840 provide a glimpse into the tactics used by gas companies against one another. On 8 October 1840, after 'several inhabitants' had asked for a supply of gas from the Commercial (LBTH, L/SGE/J/4/30, 11 November 1840), the Company succeeded in persuading the Commissioners of the St George Pavement to grant permission 'to take up the Pavements for the purposes of laying down Pipes for the supply of Gas in the District' (ibid, 8 October 1840). A deputation from the Company had met the Commissioners on the day of the meeting (ibid, 5 October 1840), stealing a march on their rivals from the Ratcliff who did not attend (ibid, letter of 22 October 1840). The Commercial lost no time in accepting the Commissioners' conditions of

payment of a £300 bond and making good the pavements within 14 days (ibid, 9 October 1840).

The decision appears to have come as a surprise to some of the Commissioners, however, who had presumably not attended the meeting. Eight of them demanded that the meeting be reconvened 'to reconsider the permission granted to the Commercial Gas Company to break the ground in St George's Parish' (LBTH, L/SGE/J/4/30, 12 October 1840). This was quickly followed by a resolution from the Trustees of the Parish of St George themselves, suggesting to the Commissioners that 'due provision be made for the supply of Gas to the public lamps' (ibid, 14 October 1840), a detail omitted from the original resolution. The advantage to parishes in granting gas companies permission to lay mains was that they received public lighting at a cheap rate, while the gas companies made their money from private consumers (Everard 1949, 100).

There is no direct evidence that the demands to reconsider and amend the original resolution were the result of arm-twisting on the part of the Ratcliff, but the Commissioners did receive a long and revealing letter from the Ratcliff's chairman, John Hammack (LBTH, L/SGE/J/4/30, 22 October 1840), on the day they held a special general meeting to discuss the decision. Hammack argued that 'permission should not be granted' to the Commercial. He stressed the loyalty of the Ratcliff, which had laid '8½ miles of Main in St George's Parish, together with 350 service pipes for the Exclusive Supply of the public lamps'. Why, he asked, 'do not the Commercial Co. lay down Mains in Bethnal Green and Limehouse, where they obtained permission some months ago'? The answer, he said, was that the Commercial was interested only in the lucrative trade of supplying private consumers and the trustees of those parishes had insisted that they should also supply gas for public lighting. He warned that if his company was forced out of business, the isolation of the parish meant that rival companies would only supply the principal streets with public light and that 'outrage and robbery' would increase.

Hammack's tone was wounded and respectful, but his implication was clear: if the Pavement Commissioners allowed the Commercial to compete, then they would be responsible for plunging the district into darkness where only criminals would flourish. Although the Commissioners' meeting on 22 October did not rescind their original decision, it did stipulate that the Commercial's mains should be sufficient to light public lamps throughout the district (LBTH, L/SGE/J/4/30, resolution of 22 October 1840). This condition was written into an agreement (much amended in the margins) drawn up between the Commissioners and the Commercial (ibid, 11 November 1840).

Even so, the Ratcliff seems ultimately to have got its way. The Commercial did not supply gas to St George's parish at this time, nor did it succeed in overcoming similar resistance from parochial bodies in Wapping and Shadwell (Maddocks 1931, 38–9). In a further blow to the Company, both the Ratcliff and the British companies dropped their prices.

The Commercial Company resorted to other means to woo

consumers and local dignitaries. In an early example of public relations, one sunny October day in 1840 Charles Green's Nassau Balloon embarked on its 278th ascent, witnessed by a multitude of local inhabitants. 'The ponderous machine with its intrepid voyagers [including the Company's engineer Isaac Mercer], rose majestically' from the 'spacious grounds' of the Company's Stepney Works (*Mechanics Mag* 1840, 384).

Its endeavours to persuade parochial authorities frustrated, the Company decided to apply for an Act of Incorporation which would give it statutory powers to lay mains. However, strong opposition from the Ratcliff, supported by the Gas Light and Coke, the British and the Imperial companies succeeded in defeating the Company's 1841 Bill (Maddocks 1931, 39). This was a heavy blow and shareholder confidence drained away – not helped by confusion in the Company's books. Shares were forfeited or sold for trifling sums; some were even liquidated in the taverns in Stepney and Whitechapel (ibid). The Company's state of collapse was exacerbated when the Poplar Company began to erect a new works with an eye on the Commercial's consumers.

A meeting of proprietors in December 1841 was crucial in turning the Company's fortunes to the good. Thirty-year-old Charles Salisbury Butler told the proprietors that with their support he and James Holbert Wilson would save the Company. He was elected chairman, with Wilson as deputy chairman, and several influential men also joined the board, including Thomas Brushfield, who had previously been an opponent of the Company. Finance was still a problem and the following year the proprietors reluctantly agreed that 3000 of the remaining shares would be subject to the payment of dividends at 5% in preference to the existing proprietors' shares, which were almost valueless. To refuse would have meant the end of the Company (Maddocks 1931, 40).

The Company turned its attention to Bethnal Green and in early 1843 Salisbury Butler's influence resulted in the parish accepting the Commercial's offer to light the public lamps. The Company also won the contract to light Limehouse, where the British Company had refused to replace the existing oil lamps with gas until the parish refused to do business with the short-lived East London Company, another rival. These were important breakthroughs. Salisbury Butler and Wilson sped to Birmingham to purchase £25,000 worth of pipes and other materials. On their return they struck a deal with the Gas Light and Coke that transferred some of its mains in Bethnal Green to the Commercial. All that was missing now was a crucial connecting main. This had to be laid on Mile End Waste (an extensive open space on Mile End Road), and since the Trustees of Whitechapel Road refused to permit the Company access to the High Street, the pipes had to be laid just outside the area of their control at Mile End Gate (Maddocks 1931, 41).

The British was determined to stop the Commercial, and as soon as the Company had laid its mains on Mile End Waste, the British dug them up. Only after the British Company's workmen had been distracted by lavish refreshments did the Commercial succeed in re-laying the mains. The British

switched tactics and applied to the Court of Chancery to commit Salisbury Butler, Wilson and the Company's engineer Isaac Mercer to prison. However, in the words of Wilson himself, 'On the evening of that very day, a day memorable in the history of the Company – 15 August 1843 – I stood with Mr [Salisbury] Butler in the High Street of Whitechapel amidst a blaze of light and amidst the acclamations of the inhabitants. Our efforts had not been in vain. From that moment our Company was established' (*J Gas Sup*, 11 April 1871, 279).

4.3 Consolidation, 1844–7

By mid 1844, the Company's gasworks consisted of retort and purifying houses and three 60ft (18.29m) diameter gasholders, with an 80ft (24.38m) diameter gasholder in the course of erection. No doubt hardened by the experiences of its turbulent early years, by 1844 the Company was taking a more professional approach to its affairs. The first dividend was declared in this year (LMA, B/CGC/2, 111 (7 July 1848)) and the Commercial again turned its attention to its registration as a public company (LMA, B/CGC/1, 94–5 (27 November 1844)).

There were changes in the internal running of the Company. In the early years, proprietors had been encouraged to attend monthly meetings to assist the directors. These meetings were held in taverns in Bethnal Green and Spitalfields and could become convivially acrimonious or worse. At least one plot to overthrow the directors was hatched (Maddocks 1931, 65). The meetings had initially helped to raise capital and influence custom, but with the number of proprietors approaching 500 the directors now considered the system detrimental. The meetings were gradually allowed to fall into abeyance and later a clause was inserted into the Company's Bill increasing the price of a share from £5 to £25 (ibid, 64–5), so reducing the potential number of smaller shareholders. Although expedient from a business point of view, the move marked a turning away from the original concept of a company run by shareholders.

General meetings of the proprietors were held twice a year at the London Tavern, Bishopsgate, in the City of London (Maddocks 1931, 65). Dividends were declared and directors elected. The press were barred from these meetings until 1855 and it was only from 1857 that proprietors were sent copies of the accounts in advance (ibid, 176). Dividends were paid at the Company's office on appointed days, which provided opportunities for contact between shareholders, who were largely consumers, and the Company (ibid, 188). However, such close relations did not always stop complaints from proprietors about the level of dividends in relation to the Company's success (LMA, B/CGC/2, 111 (7 July 1848)).

Meetings of the directors were usually held weekly on a Wednesday at the Company's offices in Stepney. The meetings heard reports from the Company's engineer, inspectors and canvassers, and considered the amount of money in the bank and the Company's liabilities. The directors decided the allocation of shares and the amount of the dividend. In the early years they were occupied with some of the minutiae of running the Company: for example, an inspector was dismissed for laying a main without permission (LMA, B/CGC/1, 3 (17 April 1844); 9 (8 May 1844)), a yard labourer was sacked for swearing at a director (ibid, 44 (31 July 1844)) and an instruction was issued that no more than 5s be spent on weekly office cleaning (ibid, 163 (23 April 1845)). Such decisions were soon delegated downwards, for example to the secretary, who was responsible for day-to-day operations, while the directors concerned themselves with the overall direction of the Company. The engineer was also a key figure, acting effectively as manager of the works as well as superintending the carbonising department, building works and machinery, and planning the route of mains (ibid, 523 (9 December 1846)).

Wilson was right to see lighting Whitechapel as a turning point. Seven out of ten inhabitants favoured the Commercial and all but one of the boards of paving commissioners modified their previous opposition (Maddocks 1931, 62). The Trustees of the Commercial Road still refused permission for the Company to lay mains, but this was circumvented at least in part by paying one householder on the road 2s 6d a year to lay pipes through his back premises to supply adjoining houses (LMA, B/CGC/1, 150 (9 April 1845)). Spitalfields became a stronghold for the Company. Ten-year contracts for supplying the public lights had been secured in the liberties of the Old Artillery Ground, Norton Folgate and the inhabited parts of Bethnal Green. The length of Brick Lane was also a core district for the Company, and another key area was the liberty of St James's Duke's Place, in the City of London on the west side of Houndsditch, where the Company also won the contract to supply the public lights (Maddocks 1931, 63). Although small – the area consisted of only 123 houses – it was later to prove an important bargaining chip in discussions with other companies. By the end of 1845, the public lighting of Mile End Old Town had been secured and the Company's pipes extended from Limehouse into Bow (ibid, 65). A year later 3300 yards (3000m) of predominantly 6in (0.15m) mains were in place in Bow parish (LMA, B/CGC/1, 297 (14 January 1846)). Also in 1846 the Company reversed years of previous failures by winning permission to lay mains in Poplar (ibid, 364 (15 April 1846)).

The price of gas plummeted as competition with the British and Ratcliff companies intensified. In September 1844 the Commercial dropped the price from 7s to 6s 6d per thousand cubic feet (LMA, B/CGC/1, 57 (28 August 1844)) and when a year later the British Company cut its own price to 6s per thousand for metered gas, the Commercial followed suit (ibid, 242–3 (3 October 1845)). There were spats with the British Company, which served writs for breach of contract on former customers who had switched to Commercial gas (ibid, 87 (6 November 1844)) and complained that the Commercial had connected its pipes to a British main (ibid, 528 (16 December 1846)).

In 1845 the Commercial's rental income for the year was just over £14,910, and a total of £2659 had been received for coke (equating to 15% of the business) and just over £81 for tar and ammoniacal liquor (0.5% of the business). Almost 65 million cubic feet of gas had been generated from 7090 tons of coal (over 9,000 cubic feet of gas per ton of coal) (LMA, B/CGC/1, 385–6 (13 May 1846)). The following year was even better and the yearly rental soared to £20,000 (Maddocks 1931, 87). With little spare capacity, the Stepney Works was struggling to meet increased demand and urgently needed to expand (LMA, B/CGC/1, 385–6 (13 May 1846)).

Consumers without meters were charged by the number of burners they used (Maddocks 1931, 62). In early 1846 the Company was charging one of its consumers, a publican, £9 per annum for four lights (LMA, B/CGC/1, 298 (14 January 1846)), and the liberty of St James Duke's Place £4 per annum for each public lamp (ibid, 301 (21 January 1846)). Discounts were occasionally available: for example Charrington Head and Company on Mile End Road were offered a 5% discount on the price of 6s per thousand cubic feet (ibid, 289 (31 December 1845)).

The success of the Commercial did not go unnoticed by other gas companies. The Independent Company, formed in 1824 and incorporated in 1829, was worried that its district in Shoreditch could be threatened. The Imperial Company, incorporated in 1821 and whose district was contiguous with Bethnal Green, was concerned about future competition in what was then rural Hackney (Maddocks 1931, 63). The Gas Light and Coke and City of London companies were alarmed by the Commercial's plans to supply their lucrative City area (ibid, 87). The British Company suffered the most from the success of its competitor. As a result the Gas Light and Coke, the capital's senior gas company, approached the Commercial's board with an offer that if the Commercial would give up lighting some areas, other companies would reciprocate (LMA, B/CGC/1, 309 (31 January 1846)). Unofficially, the pressure was more direct. At a meeting of the gas companies – ostensibly to coordinate action against dishonest consumers – Salisbury Butler said that he was told by a rival director:

that with a capital of £100,000 it was perfectly absurd for us to suppose we could go all over the Imperial district and all over the Gas Light and Coke's district; and that we had already taken £70,000 from our proprietors; that £30,000 only remained; and, therefore, how much better it would be if we were to be content with such an amount of district as we should be able with our present capital to supply. (Quoted in Maddocks 1931, 87)

The Commercial Company rejected the Gas Light and Coke's initial proposals, since they would have meant the loss of two of its most lucrative areas, Whitechapel and Stepney, which brought in a combined rental of £7330 per annum (LMA, B/CGC/1, 309 (31 January 1846)). Even so, the principle had been established that rival companies wanted a 'districting agreement' with the Commercial. The Gas Light and Coke's governor, David Pollock, persevered on behalf of his own company, the Independent and the British, and eventually a deal was reached that the Commercial would exchange some of its district for an area lit by the Gas Light and Coke. The Commercial also agreed not to 'invade' the districts of other gas companies, and in return the Gas Light and Coke and the Independent agreed to assist the Commercial in obtaining an Act of Incorporation (ibid, 340 (11 March 1846)). A copy of the final agreement was copied into the minutes of the Company a week later (ibid, 343–4 (18 March 1846)). Districting agreements were made between other companies from the mid 1850s (Everard 1949, 198).

The British Company had dropped out of the negotiations by this stage, but nevertheless attempted to make its own deal with the Commercial (LMA, B/CGC/1, 344 (18 March 1846)). The Commercial made a further agreement about its eastern boundary with the West Ham Gas Company (ibid, 425 (22 July 1846)), although this was kept secret since part of the deal was that the Commercial could light that part of West Ham then lit by the British (Maddocks 1931, 88). Even the Ratcliff came to terms, ceding the supply of part of its district, Cock Hill, and paying the Commercial £1500 to give up Goodman's Fields (ibid). It was a measure of how far the Commercial had come that rivals who had set out to ruin it a few years earlier now wanted to strike a deal about their respective spheres of activity. The Commercial was no longer an interloper, but a member of the club.

The emboldened Company declared its intention to secure an annual rental of £30,000 and instructed Mercer to draw up proposals to expand the works to achieve this goal (LMA, B/CGC/1, 455 (25 March 1846)). The Company leased 3¼ acres (1.3ha) of land north of the works, on the condition that a retort house or blue billy tank was not erected within 150ft of the new boundary (ibid, 441–2 (19 August 1846)). Two years later, the Company would buy all the land it was leasing for the Stepney Works (LMA, B/CGC/2, 141–3 (20 November 1848)).

The next stage was the Act of Incorporation itself, for which the Company resolved to apply towards the end of 1846 (LMA, B/CGC/1, 455 (9 September 1846)). Such an act would define its area of supply and give it powers to increase its capital. The Imperial Company withdrew its opposition when proposals to extend the Commercial's district into Hackney, Stoke Newington and Islington were removed (LMA, B/CGC/2, 32 (6 October 1847)). The Bill was more strenuously contested by the British and the Poplar companies. On 11 June 1847 the Commercial's board waited at Fendalls Hotel, Westminster, for the result (LMA, B/CGC/1, 605 (9 June 1847)). Relief would have swept the room when news came that the Bill had passed unopposed, reversing the failure of five years earlier.

Before the Bill became law, a preliminary inquiry into the Company was held in February 1847. This heard that the coal used was Pelaw Main, costing 6s 6d at the pit mouth and 17s delivered to the works. The 180 retorts at the 8 acre (3.2ha) Stepney Works could produce half a million cubic feet (14,158m³) of gas in 24 hours and there were plans for 90 more

retorts to be built. One ton of coal produced 9000 cubic feet (255m³) of gas and one chaldron of coke. Wet lime was the predominant method of purification, although there were plans to use dry lime too. Tar sold at 3¹/₂d and ammoniacal liquor at 2s 6d per 108 gallons. There were four gasholders (a fifth gasholder still under construction at the time of the inquiry was not included), with a capacity of a quarter of a million cubic feet (7080m³). The total length of mains and branch pipes was 45 miles 1272 yards (73.58km), on wider roads buried on each side of the footway. Gas was sold at 6s per thousand cubic feet and the Company's 528 public lamps were charged at £4 a year on average. The intensity of the light given from a burner of 5 cubic feet was equal to 12 to 14 candle power. The total number of lights was 14,313, with the shops, warehouses and public houses averaging 3¹/₂ lights each.

The Company supplied eight churches; 15 chapels; the Jews' Synagogue, Duke's Place; the Jews' Hospital, Mile End; the Town Hall, Limehouse; the Blackwall Railway Company; the Hand in Hand Asylum, St James's Place; the Truman and Company and Mann and Company breweries; the Spitalfields School of Design; ten schools; three workhouses; two police stations; and 64 factories. The bulk of the Company's customers were shops and public houses – 3105 were supplied in total, contrasting with only 35 private homes (Maddocks 1931, 89). During the inquiry, the directors claimed that the Commercial had reduced the price of gas in its district by a third, and because it treated its consumers better than its rivals and provided a better service the majority of the inhabitants were in favour of the Company (ibid, 90).

The 1847 Act empowered the Company to raise £150,000 capital by issuing 6000 £25 shares, and an additional £50,000 either by increasing the capital by subscription among existing or new shareholders or by borrowing on a mortgage. The future of the Company was assured and a feeling of security prevailed. The Act did not restrict the price of gas, its illuminating power, purity or pressure – this would eventually come in later legislation – but a maximum dividend of 10% per annum was fixed to prevent excessive profits. The Act, together with the Gas Works Clauses Act of the same year, largely freed the Company from the local boards that had caused problems previously (Maddocks 1931, 115).

As an accepted member of the group, the Commercial joined with other gas companies in defending their collective interest. An early example of this was the coordinated opposition to the Health of Towns Bill in 1847 (LMA, B/CGC/1, 589 (14 April 1847)) which sought to prevent gasworks being located in crowded residential areas (Everard 1949, 181). The Bill hardly applied to the Commercial, since its Stepney Works was on the edge of the capital, but the Gas Light and Coke and the City of London gas companies feared that their works could be compulsorily purchased by local authorities or shut down. The Bill was a response to rising consumer discontent, especially in the City, over gas price and quality. The discontent also led to the formation of the Great Central Gas Consumers' Company in 1847, which was to have a more direct effect on the Commercial.

4.4 Threats and expansion, 1848–52

The formation of the Great Central Company was a threat to all the metropolitan gas companies, but particularly the Commercial, as the new company's works was located on the Commercial's doorstep at Bow Common.

The Great Central was formed by consumers in the City of London angry that gas was charged at 7s per thousand cubic feet in their densely populated area, whereas it was only charged at 6s per thousand in districts with fewer people, such as the Commercial's. The company was led by Alexander Croll and City of London solicitor Charles Pearson, who claimed that the gas companies were keeping the price artificially high. 'Colonel' Croll was a colourful figure, a talented inventor with military pretensions (Mills 1999, 112), while Pearson was the promoter of the world's first underground railway, the Metropolitan (Ball and Sunderland 2001, 273). They promised they could supply gas at 4s per thousand and still pay annual 10% dividends. When the Great Central applied to Parliament for an Act of Incorporation it was fiercely opposed by rival companies, including the Commercial (LMA, B/CGC/2, 233 (13 February 1850)), and the Bill was rejected twice. Huge sums were lavished by the gas companies on litigation – around £30,000–£40,000 (Maddocks 1931, 117) – until eventually a modified Bill was passed in 1851.

There was no suitable place in the City for the Great Central to build its works, so instead a desolate spot at Bow Common was chosen. The £45,000 works was designed to produce 320 million cubic feet (9,061,391m³) of gas a year. To reach the City, over 2 miles (3.2 km) west, the Great Central's main would have to pass through the district supplied by the Commercial and the British companies. As it had no statutory powers at the time, the Great Central required the consent of the local boards of Whitechapel and Mile End, and obtained this by promising to supply the public lights and private consumers on the route of its main with gas at the same price as would be charged in the City (Maddocks 1931, 117).

It quickly dawned on the Commercial that such an arrangement would spell its own ruin. The Company issued a pamphlet warning its consumers 'to pause before you commit yourselves to strangers in your district' as the Great Central could provide no security beyond 'vague assurances'. Salisbury Butler even offered to have the Company's gas price regulated by the Board of Trade (NGA, NT, COG/X/X/1, c December 1849, 7–8). Meanwhile, in alliance with the Gas Light and Coke and City of London companies, the Commercial hatched plans to frustrate Croll (Maddocks 1931, 118) in what became infamous as the 'Battle of Bow Bridge'.

In August 1850, when contractors from the Great Central tried to lay their pipes over one of the Regent's Canal bridges, labourers from the Commercial appeared and drove them away. Reinforced by 200 men (Everard 1949, 186) – nominally from the Commercial, but actually also from other gas companies (Maddocks 1931, 118) – the Commercial laid its own pipes across the crown of the bridge and across each end to block the route of the Great Central's main. By law, if the Commercial's pipes stayed in the ground for three days, only Parliament could legally remove them (Everard 1949, 186).

The Great Central rallied, and in the early hours of the following morning marched 300 hired labourers 'in martial array, armed with pickaxes, shovels, and other implements to the scene of action, preceded by a wagon drawn by three horses' (*The Times*, 9 August 1850, 7). Meanwhile, another group marched from Stepney in a flanking manoeuvre. Once at the bridge, the wagon and horses were driven at speed towards a 10ft (3.05m) barricade erected by the Commercial. Several men were knocked down, two fell in the canal and one was hospitalised after his legs were crushed under the wagon. Further disaster was averted only when police arrested one of the Commercial's officers before he could set fire to gas issuing from one of the mains.

Despite being as well armed as the Great Central's labourers, the Commercial's men were driven back by superior numbers. As much of Stepney's population looked on, the Great Central took possession of the bridge. The Commercial's secretary, George Jaques, was arrested and subsequently remanded for knocking over two men himself (*The Times*, 9 August 1850, 7) and for trying to prevent the parish's beadle from taking a shovel to the Commercial's pipes (Everard 1949, 186).

A large force of police got between the two sides to stop the fighting. Although the Commercial's men gathered in local pubs for a counter-attack, there were only minor skirmishes once even more police reinforcements arrived. The Great Central's labourers barricaded the bridge and replaced the Commercial's mains with its own (*The Times*, 9 August 1850, 7). Croll had won the day, and his victory was even celebrated in poetry (Mills 1999, 108). A crestfallen George Jaques appeared before the Commercial's board a few days later to explain the defeat (LMA, B/CGC/2, 274–5 (14 August 1850)).

The Great Central's victory forced the Commercial to cut the price of its gas first from 6s to 5s per thousand cubic feet (LMA, B/CGC/2, 245 (2 April 1850)) and then to 4s per thousand (ibid, 286, 25 September 1850)). The Company initially attempted to maintain 4s only along the Great Central's main, but the lower price was extended throughout the district after consumers complained, and the Commercial reached agreement with the Whitechapel and Mile End Old Town trustees to light the public lamps in those parishes. Other gas companies threatened by the Great Central, such as the Gas Light and Coke and the City of London companies, also dropped their prices (Everard 1949, 182). The struggle with the Great Central cost the Commercial its superintendent, who was compelled to resign because of his association with Croll. In a *volte face* that angered his former allies at the Gas Light and Coke and City companies, Salisbury Butler proposed that the Commercial amalgamate with the Great Central (ibid, 187). Better news came in 1851, when the Great Central's Act precluded that company from supplying the Commercial's district (Maddocks 1931, 119).

Croll's management skills were not good: the Great Central Gas Works quickly fell into chaos and bad practice, and the company was prosecuted for nuisance (Mills 1999, 112). Eventually the Great Central Company was subsumed into the Gas Light and Coke in 1870 (below, 4.6).

At the end of 1850, a strike loomed at the Stepney Works. What motivated the foreman and stokers to threaten to leave their work is not clear from the Minute Books (LMA, B/CGC/2, 297 (20 November 1850)), although the *Co-Partnership Herald* implies that the Great Central was behind it (Maddocks 1931, 118). Perhaps the Company's stokers were encouraged by their success four years earlier when they asked for a pay rise and received an increase to 26s a week (LMA, B/CGC/1, 428 (29 July 1846)). Then, the Company may have wanted to avoid the fate of the Gas Light and Coke, whose Westminster Works had suffered a strike that year inspired by the Chartist movement (Everard 1949, 124). What is clear, however, is that the Company took a hard line this time. The board empowered the secretary 'to adopt such Measures as the urgency of the Case demands'. Additional gasholder capacity was provided and help sought from other metropolitan companies. The use of labour supplied from other gas companies to break strikes had been a successful tactic elsewhere (ibid, 123).

In the event, 'several daring attempts [were made] to injure the Company's property' (LMA, B/CGC/2, 298 (25 November 1850)). The police were called and many of the Company's men had to be forcibly driven out of the works (Maddocks 1931, 118). Later, the board extended its thanks to the Gas Light and Coke, Ratcliff, Phoenix, British and City of London companies 'for their friendly and most efficient assistance' – presumably in putting their own men at the disposal of the Commercial (LMA, B/CGC/2, 297 (25 November 1850)). A new foreman was appointed and it is safe to assume that the strikers were dismissed. The Company paid two police inspectors a guinea each for their extra services (ibid, 309 (15 January 1851)).

Expansion had been on the Company's mind for a few years. The Company had considered building a new works at Stratford (LMA, B/CGC/1, 262 (12 November 1845)) and on the Isle of Dogs (LMA, B/CGC/2, 25 (15 September 1847)). However, in the end the board decided to buy the Poplar Company's works for £12,000. The Poplar Company had originally offered to sell the Commercial its works in 1847 (Maddocks 1931, 89). Incorporated in 1821, the Poplar was in poor shape and had struggled for most of its existence in a tiny district comprising Poplar parish and a small part of Bromley. Its 50 shareholders had forgone dividends to keep the company afloat, but mismanagement, poor supply and competition – not least from the Commercial – were proving a fatal combination (ibid, 116). The Commercial took possession of the company's Poplar and Isle of Dogs stations in late 1849 (LMA, B/CGC/2, 225 (26 December 1849)) and by the following May the Poplar Company's district was being supplied by the Stepney Works (ibid, 255 (22 May 1850)).

Another of the Commercial's rivals was also beginning to totter. An argument erupted with the British Company when the Commercial won a contract to supply Charrington and Co, a large brewery in Mile End, at the then hugely discounted rate

of 4s per thousand. The British was furious, accusing the Commercial of acting in an underhand manner and of breaching an agreement between the two companies. The Commercial claimed that the move was to prevent the Great Central from supplying Charringtons and was in the interests of the British because it would be the Commercial that bore the loss of profit from the discounted rate. In a fine twist of logic, the Commercial told the British that 'no underhand proceedings ever would be sanctioned by them [the Commercial's board] and therefore none have taken place' (LMA, B/CGC/2, 256–8 (22 May 1850)).

In September 1851, a key meeting of directors from both the Commercial and British agreed that two companies competing in the same area could not hope to make a profit while the reduced price of gas persisted (Maddocks 1931, 140). The reality was that competition with the Commercial was crippling the British (Everard 1949, 105). A few weeks later the British was offering to sell its 'Land, Shares, Gas Works, Property, Gear and other effects' in London to the Commercial (LMA, B/CGC/2, 369 (17 October 1851)) which the Commercial bought for the knockdown price of £65,000 (Everard 1949, 105; Maddocks 1931, 142). The British Company had entered the district in 1824 and established its chief works at Schoolhouse Lane, Ratcliff, before embarking on a price war with its bitter opponents, the Ratcliff Company. In 1829, the same year it was incorporated, the British acquired another works at Old Ford Road, near Bow Church, in a deal with the Imperial which saw the British gain control of the gas supply of Whitechapel, Mile End, Stepney, Bow, West Ham and Wellclose Square. The company built up support in the parochial boards, but neglect of its consumers had prompted the formation of the Commercial (ibid, 140–2). Now the British decided to quit the capital in favour of its rival and concentrate on providing gas in the provinces (Everard 1949, 105).

The Parliamentary bill authorising the sale to the Commercial received royal assent in July 1852 (LMA, B/CGC/3, 89 (2 July 1852)) and the transfer was complete by October (ibid, 130 (19 October 1852)). The new Act also allowed the Commercial to increase its capital from £200,000 to £450,000 and extended its district to West Ham parish, in which the Company later sold its interests to the West Ham Company for £6924. The Commercial also gained another asset in the person of the British Company's William Christie, who became a director. Christie was deputy chairman of the Commissioners of Sewers in the City of London as well as a powerful figure in Bow, where he lived (Maddocks 1931, 142–3).

The Commercial also eliminated another potential rival. It offered £600 to purchase the gasworks of the North Woolwich Land Company (LMA, B/CGC/2, 368 (17 October 1851); LMA, B/CGC/3, 33 (30 January 1852)). Initially the offer was declined, but when the Company finally bought the works it was sold off in September 1853 (LMA, B/CGC/3, 286 (16 September 1853)).

The Company's influence and power were increasing. In

1852 the chairman, Charles Salisbury Butler, was elected MP for Tower Hamlets, which he represented until 1868 (Maddocks 1931, 143).

4.5 Modernisation, 1852–9

In disposing of its new property and assets, the Company was careful that no competitor should benefit. The British Company's wharf at Cock Hill and estate in Brook Street were sold for £7025. Use of the works in Schoolhouse Lane, Ratcliff, which included five gasholders ranging from 37ft (11.28m) to 49ft (14.94m) in diameter, was discontinued in 1855, and what could not be sold off was allowed to fall into disrepair or put out of action. At the end of the lease in 1860 the premises were surrendered to the landlord with the pipes dug up, the tanks filled in and the ground stripped bare. The roof of the retort house was so dilapidated that it collapsed under the weight of snow that winter (Maddocks 1931, 173).

The works acquired from the Poplar Company on the Isle of Dogs was also discontinued, and its gasholder sold (LMA, B/CGC/3, 536 (16 March 1855)). The works at Bow was closed and its two gasholders were purchased by the Crystal Palace District Gas Company for £560 (LMA, B/CGC/4, 35 (5 June 1857); Maddocks 1931, 174) and by the Tottenham Gas Company for £200 (Co-partnership H, 11 December 1857, 72).

Meanwhile, the Company's own Stepney Works was being rebuilt (see below) by its new engineer, Robert Jones, who was appointed in 1854. The Company divided its area of supply into four districts (1 to 4), roughly west to east. A rental of £62,672 12s was being brought in from a total of 9626 consumers (loose sheet in LMA, B/CGC/4, 74 (24 December 1857)). The mains also needed renewal, especially those acquired from the British Company. At least some of the mains work was contracted out to Aird and Sons, who were engaged to lay a 14in (0.36m) pipe from Bancroft Place to Bow (LMA, B/CGC/4, 28 (1 May 1857); 31 (15 May 1857)). The Company also considered the practicality of using cast iron service pipes (LMA, B/CGC/3, 384 (28 April 1854)). Mains renewal was spread over several years until Jones could announce to the proprietors in 1861 that the mains 'are as perfect as they can be' (quoted in Maddocks 1931, 174). In 1856 the loss of gas was estimated as 35% and in 1861 as 19% (although the 1856 figure includes a major fracture of a main at West India Docks) (ibid, 175).

The parochial authorities were also undergoing change, with the powers of the old lighting commissioners transferred by the Metropolis Management Act of 1855 to district boards, representing groups of small hamlets and parishes, and to vestries, in parishes of sufficient size and importance. Within the Company's district were the district boards of Whitechapel, Limehouse and Poplar and the vestries of Mile End and Bethnal Green. Each of these elected bodies sent one member to the new Metropolitan Board of Works (Maddocks 1931, 190).

By the late 1850s, 12-month contracts were being made to supply coke to large industrial users, for example to the London and North Western Railway (LMA, B/CGC/4, 28 (24 April 1857)) and the London Dock Company (ibid, 64 (30 October 1857)), reflecting the interdependence of industry as it developed in the capital. Such consumers were a lucrative market, and the Commercial even supplied the Victoria Docks Gas Company with bulk supplies of gas. This company was formed in 1858, buying the North Woolwich Gas Company as a going concern, but even though it opened a new works in 1864 it could not cope with peak demand from its many industrial firms (Everard 1949, 241). Annual contracts made securing sufficient coal a key priority and much time was expended by the Commercial's board in 1857, for example, in acquiring the 50,000 tons needed for the forthcoming year (LMA, B/CGC/4, 32 (22 May 1857)).

In 1858, the Commercial's engineer reported 'the disaffected state of the Stokers upon the Company's Works and that several of them had left the Works' (LMA, B/CGC/4, 135 (3 December 1858)) (Fig 18). The crisis was over a few days later (ibid, 137 (10 December 1858)) and led to an increase in wages of 1s a week when it was found that the Commercial paid less than other companies (ibid, 138 (17 December 1858)). Other changes to the stokers' conditions included the erection of a 'lobby and dining room' for their use (ibid, 167 (8 July 1859)) and 'a treat' – a day out in the country – which was the practice at other gas companies (ibid, 171 (15 July 1859)).

The following year the Company's workers threatened to strike again (LMA, B/CGC/4, 173 (29 July 1859)) in sympathy with those of other metropolitan gas companies. The strikers had combined under the name of the Loyal Gas Stokers' Protection Society and demanded increased wages and a reduction in working hours. Strikes hit the works of the Gas Light and Coke, Imperial, and Great Central companies, threatening to plunge London into darkness (Maddocks 1931, 222). The strike at the Gas Light and Coke's Westminster Works lasted four months and ended with a new workforce being brought in to replace union members who had been sacked (Everard 1949, 201). At the Stepney Works, an increase in the height of the wall on the south side of the works near the canal was reputed by some to have been the reason the Commercial men stayed at their posts, since it separated them from the stokers, firemen and others from the Great Central's works who arrived to encourage them to join the strike (Maddocks 1931, 223).

When they appeared before the magistrate, the five ringleaders of the 52 Great Central strikers faced up to three months' hard labour for their actions (which included burning an effigy of their manager at Bow Common). However, in the event they were fined a week's wages (The Times, 4 August 1859, 11), although they almost certainly lost their employment in the gas industry too. At the Commercial, as a result of the unrest a 'Benefit Society for the Company's Workmen' was established, to which the Company donated £100 a year (Maddocks 1931, 223; LMA, B/CGC/4, 185–6 (14 October 1859)).

Fig 18 A double hand-stoking gang at Stepney c 1892 – left to right, back row: J Bovrill, S Deaves, W Deaves, H Whittington, A Deamer and H Parlour; front row: W Wood, T Whybrow, N Spooner, E Isles, C Tassels, D Davey and A Owen (Co-partnership H, October 1932, 190)

4.6 New legislation and the Stokers' Strike, 1860–74

The final six months of 1860 were more prosperous than any before (Maddocks 1931, 224). Output reached new highs – in one night in 1860 3 million cubic feet (*c* 85,000m³) of gas were generated. Although gas was still mainly supplied for public lamps and business premises, the general adoption of gas in private houses taking place across the metropolis was also affecting the Commercial's district, albeit at a slower rate, as there were fewer private residences of well-to-do people (ibid, 223). In the 1860s gas was claimed to be 30 times cheaper than wax candles (Clegg 1866, 94).

For 1861, it was estimated that the Company made over £29,000 profit exclusive of interest, and brought in almost £95,000 from gas rental (6.7% of the total brought in by London's 13 gas companies that year) and over £21,000 from sale of residuals (18.4% of the business). The cost of coal was almost £52,000 that year, with the Company producing 598 million cubic feet (16,933,474m³) of gas, which was 7.5% of the total volume of gas produced in London (Colburn 1865, 84).

The 1860s marked a time when legislation was used to rationalise the gas industry and bring it more under public control. The most important Act of the decade, the Metropolis Gas Act of 1860, marked a new era for the gas industry in London. Three years earlier, gas companies north of the Thames had negotiated the exchange of districts and the

withdrawal of some companies where competition had existed before. Such arrangements had already taken place in south London without controversy. However, the establishment of these new monopolies prompted a public outcry. The formation of a Gas Consumers' Mutual Protection Association and bitter attacks on the administration of the gas industry did not go unnoticed by the government (Maddocks 1931, 189), which ordered an inquiry that led eventually to the passing of the 1860 Act.

The 1860 Metropolis Gas Act introduced controls on London gas companies to prevent abuse of their monopolies, while at the same time recognising the advantages of each company having a non-competitive area of supply which would reduce the cost of gas distribution and the nuisance of rival companies continually digging up streets for mains (Fig 19). The provisions of the Act were not onerous for the gas companies, whose successful opposition had effectively emasculated it. The legislation, which formalised the districts already agreed by the companies, limited dividends to 10%, and stipulated a maximum price of 5s 6d per thousand cubic feet for coal gas and 7s 6d for the richer cannel gas (at a time when the maximum prices were 4s 6d and 6s respectively). It introduced the independent testing of gas, but at standards of purity and candle power that were not hard to meet (Everard 1949, 200). A medical officer from Whitechapel District tested illuminating power at the Stepney Works (LMA, B/CGC/4, np (9 March 1860)).

Another important piece of legislation, which the Commercial joined other metropolitan companies in opposing,

Fig 19 A main laying gang c *1899 – left to right: 'Sarah' Davy, James Harvey, Fred Seymour, George Hollis (whose son and father also worked at Stepney),*
Peter Mason (who had a grandson at the works), Jack Foster (who had a nephew at the works), A J Bowyer (a night watchman at Stepney) and R Richardson
(Co-partnership H, *December 1932, 238*)

was the Corporation of London's Bill (LMA, B/CGC/6, 165 (31 January 1868)), intended to give the Corporation the power to compulsorily purchase gas companies supplying the City. The Metropolitan Board of Works was also actively in favour of such powers for itself in the rest of London (Everard 1949, 230). When the Corporation's Bill passed into law as 'an Act to amend the Metropolis Gas Act, 1860, and to make further provision for regulating the supply of Gas to the City of London', it had been shorn of its compulsory purchase powers, but it fixed the maximum price of gas for companies supplying the City at 4s per thousand cubic feet for 14 candle power gas until the end of 1869 and thereafter at 3s 9d for 16 candle power gas, and set dividends at a maximum of 10%. The 1868 Act also made amalgamations of companies considerably simpler (ibid, 233–4), something that would have far reaching consequences the following decade.

With the threat of compulsory purchase removed, the gas industry in London continued to be concentrated in private hands. Elsewhere, local authorities were empowered to take over local gas undertakings, and this occurred largely in Lancashire, Yorkshire and the Midlands from 1875 (Stewart 1958, 43).

The 1868 legislation spurred the development of purification. Official tests by 'gas referees' were coordinated by 1868, and gas testing was extended to the whole country by the Gas Works Clauses Act of 1871. Penalties were levied if the gas

did not meet the stipulated illuminating power, or was not free from ammonia or hydrogen sulphide, or contained more than the permitted sulphur compounds. The test for sulphur compounds led to a reversion, in part, to the use of dry lime in purification (Stewart 1958, 25). In 1905 the law governing the amount of permissible sulphur compounds was relaxed for London companies (later elsewhere) and the use of lime faded out by 1912, to be replaced completely by iron oxide (ibid, 26).

The engineer's report in 1870 to the Commercial's board about the City of London Gas Act 1868 and the Company's ability to meet the clauses relating to illuminating power is explored in more detail in Chapter 5. Whereas the Metropolis Gas Act of 1860 largely formalised a situation that was already in place (in terms of districting arrangements), the 1868 legislation, combined with rising demand for the Company's gas, was a driving factor behind a reconstruction of the Stepney Works that took place from 1870. The board was aware that the modernisation of the works would not only meet the requirement of the Act, but would improve the Company's balance sheet. It recognised that to offset the higher standard for illuminating power and the resultant increasing use by the Company of expensive cannel coal to enrich the gas, combined with the reduction in the price of gas, the works had to be as efficient as possible (LMA, B/CGC/8, 34–6 (25 February 1870)). By 1872 Jones was reporting that there was an 'unprecedented increase in the consumption of Gas over the whole of the

Company's district during the last two years' and this required 'immediate steps' (ibid, 166–8 (8 November 1872)).

Costs were also rising. Fees for conveying coal by barge were an increasing concern, and the secretary and engineer investigated whether there were any other means of getting coal to the works (LMA, B/CGC/4, np (9 March 1860)). The Regent's Canal Company was charging an additional 2d per ton of coal (ibid, np (5 April 1860)), a considerable amount considering the Company was bringing in tens of thousands of tons of coal a year.

By the mid 1860s the Company was using a large amount of cannel coal to enrich the gas and give it an illuminating power of 14^1/$_2$ candles (LMA, B/CGC/6, 146–7 (23 August 1867)). A sharp increase in the price of coal in the early 1870s (Everard 1949, 246) also proved expensive for the Company as coal consumption at the works rose. In August 1870, for example, the Commercial ordered 64,500 tons of North Pelton gas coal (LMA, B/CGC/8, 56 (5 August 1870)).

London's gas industry was changing. In 1868 the Gas Light and Coke began to build the world's biggest gasworks in east London. The first pile was driven in by Simon Beck, the Gas Light and Coke's governor, and the company's property was renamed Beckton in his honour (Everard 1949, 234–5). Gas making began at Beckton two years later (ibid, 239). By 1878 the Gas Light and Coke's land covered c 150 acres (60ha), almost 20 times the size of the Commercial's Stepney Works. A railway system connected with the Great Eastern Company's line, there was a model village for workers and their families including a church and a company school, and a chemical works was under construction. All but 800 of the 2000 people employed at the Beckton Works toiled in the carbonising department, the hand-charged retorts capable of generating 25 million cubic feet (707,921m^3) of gas a day (ibid, 265–6). The twelfth retort house was added in early 1883 (ibid, 253). Most of the nine huge gasholders shown on the 1896 Ordnance Survey map (not illustrated) had been built by the late 1870s, and these fed the 48in (1.22m) main running to the City and Westminster.

Beckton was not the only giant works constructed in this period. The Imperial Company built a works at Bow Creek, Bromley-by-Bow, although compared with Beckton it was obsolescent from the start. With old-fashioned gasholders and no direct river access for coal supply, it was a £300,000 white elephant (Everard 1949, 237, 246, 254). Over the river, the South Metropolitan Company built its own 150 acre (60ha) East Greenwich Works in the 1880s (Tucker 2000, 18). In general the large works, built on cheap land with riverside facilities for coal deliveries, produced significant economies of scale which, combined with escalating demand for gas, managed to offset the increasing price of raw materials such as coal in the late 1870s.

The implications of the rising demand for gas were not lost on the Commercial's workmen and their 1871 petition to the board, via the engineer, resulted in an increase in pay (LMA, B/CGC/8, 123 (8 December 1871)). A general agitation for shorter hours and increased pay by gas workers from all companies continued into 1872 (Everard 1949, 244). The demand for shorter hours extended beyond the gas industry,

and there were strikes of colliers, agricultural workers and bakers, with the 'contagion of strikes' even spreading to the Metropolitan Police (*The Times*, 31 December 1872, 6).

The Stokers' Strike began in December 1872. Three months earlier, the chairmen and deputy chairmen of several metropolitan gas companies met to approve a scale of workers' wages that had been proposed by their engineers, and agreed 'to make no advance beyond such rates without previous conference with the whole of the Companies' (LMA, B/CGC/8, 159 (13 September 1872)). In fact, the men of the 'Commercial, Pimlico, Westminster, Beckton and Bow stations' rejected the proposed scale, and an improved one was devised in which firemen and scoopmen would be paid 38s 9d, stokers 37s 4d and barrowmen 31s for seven days' work. The companies' belief that the new rates 'would be satisfactory to the men' (ibid) would prove to be misplaced.

The background to the unprecedented December strike was given by Harry Chubb, the secretary of the Imperial Company, who wrote to *The Times* to complain that there had been a growing spirit of insubordination since a 'Stokers' Union' had been established the previous September; workers at the Imperial had gone on strike the following month. The December dispute was sparked by the sacking of a labourer, employed to carry coke at the Imperial's Fulham Works, who had refused an order. His colleagues refused to start work until he was reinstated, so the Imperial replaced them with non-union labour they had already procured. In the next two days the strike spread to the St Pancras and the Haggerston works, where the workers were replaced in the same way as their colleagues at Fulham (*The Times*, 4 December 1872, 5).

The focus then shifted to the Gas Light and Coke's giant Beckton Works, which employed some 1200 men at the time, two-thirds of them in the retort houses. At the handover between the night and day shifts, 500 men gathered and demanded that Thomas Dilley, who had been sacked ten days earlier, be reinstated and that the lock-out at Fulham be ended. The men walked out after the Gas Light and Coke's superintendent agreed to reinstate Dilley 'under protest', but said he could do nothing about the situation in the works of another company (*The Times*, 20 December 1872, 11). The strike continued to spread until all but one of the capital's gasworks were out, including the Commercial's Stepney Works.

A meeting of the strikers in the Bell and Bull Inn, Finsbury, a day into the strike heard reports from each of the works about progress. Mr C Beams, a delegate from the Stepney Works, reported that '15 blacklegs had gone in there; 150 men remained out' (*The Times*, 4 December 1872, 5). Many years later the Company's in-house magazine put the number of strikers at 100 (*Co-partnership H*, March 1931, 9).

The 'monstrous attempt to inflict a plague of darkness on the metropolis' (*The Times*, 6 December 1872, 10) resulted in London's gas supply being interrupted for about a week (ibid, 31 December 1872, 6). It was broken by the companies using outside labour to replace the strikers. *The Times* reported that 'the whole of the Metropolitan Police received orders from Scotland Yard to send down as many labourers as they could to the gasworks where strikes exist' and in the Commercial's district, when the Mile End Old Town Vestry complained that many of their public lamps were not lit, the Company issued a plea that the vestry's own men help out at the works (ibid, 6 December 1872, 10). Later, the board thanked the vestry and Aird and Sons, who had built coal lifting apparatus at the works earlier that year, for their 'valuable assistance' during the strike, and gave the engineer £100 to distribute at his discretion (LMA, B/CGC/8, 172–3 (6 December 1872)).

The Gas Light and Coke issued summonses against all 500 Beckton strikers for breaching the Master and Servants Act 1867 (*The Times*, 6 December 1872, 10), which stipulated that workers in breach of contract could be imprisoned (Galenson 1994, 127). Dilley and four others were found guilty of conspiracy at the Old Bailey and sentenced to 12 months' imprisonment (*The Times*, 20 December 1872, 11). The Commercial also prosecuted four of its own workers under the Act: 'Brown, Dixon, Mortimer and Rous' (LMA, B/CGC/8, 172–3 (6 December 1872)). The board ignored the pleas of a Miss Wheeler who urged them to intervene on behalf of Rouse [*sic*], a stoker whom the magistrate had imprisoned for six weeks, and circulated the names of all the strikers to the other metropolitan companies (ibid, 174 (13 December 1872)).

Sunday working was still an issue, but when the stokers petitioned the engineer about this in 1873, he informed them after consulting with other companies that this would be dispensed with where practicable. He added that he could not pay them 1½ days' wages for Sunday working (LMA, B/CGC/8, 194 (9 May 1873)). Industrial unrest evidently continued to simmer. Two years later the board ordered that a copy of Section 4 of the Conspiracy and Protection of Property Act 1875 should be placed in the stokers' lobby (LMA, B/CGC/10, 103 (17 September 1875)). This section of the Act made breaches of contract of employment – for example by striking – by workers in the gas, water or electricity industries illegal (Bar-Niv 1979, 250).

As well as the construction of large gasworks and the strike, the 1870s were characterised by a series of amalgamations. In 1870, the Gas Light and Coke Company amalgamated with the City of London Gas Company, the Great Central Company and the Victoria Docks Gas Company (Everard 1949, 237–40). The Equitable Gas Company was next in 1871 and the Western Gas Company the following year (ibid, 242). In 1872 the Ratcliff Company approached the Gas Light and Coke about amalgamation, but on terms the Gas Light and Coke could not accept, and the Ratcliff amalgamated with the Commercial three years later instead (ibid, 242).

The Gas Light and Coke's policy of general amalgamation continued in 1876 when it amalgamated with the huge Imperial Company and the Independent Company, conceding a 'sliding scale' by which a rising gas price meant a falling dividend. The Gas Light and Coke now dwarfed the Commercial, its area of supply spanning the whole of London north of the Thames apart from the Commercial's district and parts of Westminster, Chelsea and Fulham, which were served by the London Company (Everard 1949, 247). Flushed with its success, the Gas

Light and Coke approached the South Metropolitan, Phoenix and Surrey Consumers' companies on the south side of the river about amalgamation, but was rebuffed (ibid, 248).

Although it is not explicit, there is the sense from the Commercial's minutes that there were intense discussions in the boardroom about how the Company should react to the changing landscape of the capital's gas industry in this period. The Commercial had itself considered amalgamation with the Imperial Company four years before the latter merged with the Gas Light and Coke (LMA, B/CGC/8, 146 (21 June 1872)). The Gas Light and Coke approached the Commercial about amalgamation in 1871 (Everard 1949, 242; LMA, B/CGC/8, 91 (28 April 1871)) and 1873 (LMA, B/CGC/8, 207 (1 August 1873)), but was rejected both times – in 1871 because the board was not convinced the move would provide the proprietors with 'their statutory dividend of 10%' (ibid, 91 (28 April 1871)). The board agonised over merger with the Gas Light and Coke, considered the Commercial's 'natural allies' at the time, especially as its main from Beckton ran through the Company's district (ibid, 166–8 (8 November 1872)). Nevertheless, a third approach was rejected in 1883 (LMA, B/CGC/14, 116 (31 August 1883)), the same year that the Gas Light and Coke amalgamated with the London Gas Light Company (Everard 1949, 261).

In 1873 the board resolved 'to avoid all idea of amalgamation with any Company' (LMA, B/CGC/8, 190 (28 March 1873)), although this did not prevent the merger with the Ratcliff two years later. Instead of amalgamation, the Company decided to 'consider the erection of additional works elsewhere' (ibid), for example at Bromley (ibid, 205 (25 July 1873)). A new works was needed because by 1872 the Stepney Works had no reserve power in the carbonising department and the Company was suffering from 'too much trade, without the means as regards capital and land to meet it' according to the engineer (ibid, 166–8 (8 November 1872)). The Company purchased 11½ acres (4.7ha) for £27,716 at Bromley to build its new Poplar Works, with an option to purchase a further 8½ acres (3.4ha; ibid, 212 (5 September 1873)). More land was bought in 1876 and construction of the Company's first gasholder began that year (references to LMA, B/CGC/10, for November 1873, January 1874, and January and March 1876, given in Tucker 2000, 91). Three huge gasholders were built at the Poplar Works: a two lift holder (no. 1) of 1.5 million cubic feet (42,475m^3) capacity, in 1876–7; in 1880–2 a holder similar in form (no. 2) but of over double the capacity; and in 1928–9 a four lift gasholder (no. 3) of 4 million cubic feet (113,267m^3) capacity (Tucker 2000, 92–3). An additional retort house and purifying house were built in the mid 1880s (LMA, B/CGC/14, 195 (9 May 1884)). Originally intended to supplement the Stepney Works, Poplar was to become the Company's only production facility when Stepney closed in 1945 (Chapter 5.7).

Charles Salisbury Butler died in 1870, 'a great loss' (LMA, B/CGC/8, 68 (25 November 1870)). He had been chairman for almost 30 years and had piloted the Company through its early turbulent years into stability. James Holbert Wilson, who succeeded him as chairman, called his friend the Company's founder and praised his 'indomitable perseverance which enabled him to overcome all the impediments in the way of the first formation of this Company' (*J Gas Sup*, 11 April 1871, 279).

4.7 Mass unionism and the rise of electricity, 1875–99

The last quarter of the 19th century saw prices drop and demand rise fast. Between 1874 and 1888, for example, the gas produced by London works increased by 87% (Ball and Sunderland 2001, 274) and by 1882 the annual national output of gas was 65,000 million cubic feet (some 1,841 million cubic metres) (Stewart 1958, 44). The gas industry was increasingly subject to legislation, with companies opposing or accepting proposed laws according to how they affected their interests. Bills laid before Parliament included the Metropolis Gas Purchases Bill (LMA, B/CGC/10, 73 (19 February 1875)), the Gas Regulations Bill (ibid, 82 (9 April 1875)), the Corporation Gas Bill (LMA, B/CGC/13, 17 (2 January 1880); 85 (28 May 1880)), and the London Government Bill (LMA, B/CGC/14, 195 (9 May 1884)).

The Commercial's own new Act of Parliament was passed in 1875 (LMA, B/CGC/10, 96 (23 July 1875)), and although the Company now had to submit to a sliding scale it avoided the costly 'auction clauses' to which other companies were subjected by later legislation. The 1875 Act allowed vital capital to be raised to fund the expansion of the Poplar Works; at the same time high dividends were paid to shareholders (*J Gas Sup*, 6 April 1880, 510). The Act also allowed the amalgamation with the Ratcliff Company, agreed the previous year (LMA, B/CGC/10, np (4 February 1876)). The Ratcliff's difficulties included the fact that its capital was exhausted as a result of the fall in the price of gas from 4s to 3s 9d per thousand cubic feet (LMA, B/CGC/8, 166–8 (8 November 1872)). The advantages of the merger to the Commercial included the acquisition of the Wapping Works: bought by the Ratcliff Company in 1835, this was located on Wapping High Street and had important river access for coal deliveries (Ridge 1998, 2). Once the 1875 Act was passed, Ratcliff directors took their seats on the Commercial's board at the first meeting in the new year of 1876.

As part of the regime of testing, a gas testing station was established at Wellclose Square, Poplar (LMA, B/CGC/10, np (24 March 1876)) and later others were set up elsewhere, for example in Parnell Road, Old Ford (LMA, B/CGC/14, 98 (13 July 1883)). The chief gas examiner made regular reports, and gas referees were empowered by the Metropolis Gas Act 1860 to test for hydrogen sulphide and ammonia as well as illuminating power. The maximum amount of sulphur allowed by the referees was 30 grains per 100 cubic feet (LMA, B/CGC/10, np (6 April 1877)) and this standard became even more stringent by the beginning of the 1880s (LMA, B/CGC/13, 216 (11 March 1881)). In 1884 the Company was

fined 40s for supplying gas half a candle below the minimum illuminating power standard. The Commercial had the dubious honour of being the first gas company to be so penalised since the standard was established in 1875 (LMA, B/CGC/14, 295–6 (27 February 1885); *J Gas Sup*, 24 February 1885, 334).

By the late 1870s some in the gas industry began to fear that the emerging electricity industry would threaten their business. Gas companies even experimented with the 'rival illuminant' themselves, but found that electric light exhibited the same disadvantages as gaslight had done 70 years earlier – an offensive smell, unnatural brilliance, and the propensity to cause headaches (Everard 1949, 262). The weakness and fragmented nature of the electricity industry in London (Ball and Sunderland 2001, 277) also seem to have alleviated the gas companies' fears, and it was not until 1882 that gas companies took the threat seriously and opposed the first Electric Lighting Bill and the private bills of a number of electricity companies (Everard 1949, 263). Competition between the gas and electricity companies began in earnest in the 1890s (Stewart 1958, 44).

In the Commercial's district, electricity companies made very advantageous offers to the Whitechapel and Poplar district boards of works and to large consumers like the London Hospital and breweries. The Commercial's engineer, who was unconvinced that electricity would have a significant impact on the gas industry, told these consumers – undoubtedly with his tongue in his cheek – that the cheapest way of obtaining electric light would be to install dynamos driven by engines powered by the Commercial's gas (LMA, B/CGC/17, 286 (1 June 1899)).

Nonetheless, like other gas companies, by the 1880s the Commercial was exploring ways to increase gas use and thus offset the threat from electricity. The board resolved 'that it is expedient to stimulate the Consumption of Gas by letting Gas Engines, Stoves and other Apparatus for hire' (LMA, B/CGC/13, 343 (13 January 1882)). Initially it was cautious about this new business direction, and even sought legal opinion about whether the Company had the necessary powers (ibid, 343–4 (13 January 1882)). However, the board was soon reassured and a few months later a circular was distributed to the Company's consumers outlining the terms for the hire of 'Cooking and Heating Stoves' (ibid, 416 (28 July 1882)). Thereafter the Company regularly contributed to various exhibitions of gas stoves and other appliances (eg LMA, B/CGC/15, 121 (25 February 1887)).

The Commercial was also taking advantage of emergent technology. 'Telephone instruments and communicating line' were set up between the Company and its shipping agent in 1886 (LMA, B/CGC/15, 56 (27 August 1886)). Such instruments evidently came in useful and in 1893 the Company agreed to pay £17 a year to be put on the National Telephone Company system for five years (LMA, B/CGC/16, 391–2 (7 December 1893)).

The late 1880s saw a surge of new mass unionism across industry. It was in London that Will Thorne (a worker at Beckton Gasworks) and Eleanor Marx (Karl Marx's daughter) set up what was to become the National Union of Gas Workers and General Labourers (Ball and Sunderland 2001, 275). In the summer of 1889, the Commercial's board received a petition signed by members of the 'Commercial Branch of the Gas Workers Union' including its secretary, James Monk. The petition, passed by 'a largely attended meeting of Stokers and Gasworkers' from the Company, said that the increase in work due to the greater quantity of coal being carbonised was jeopardising the workers' health and family life because men were away from home for 13 or 14 hours a day. The petition demanded an eight-hour day and a reduction in work (LMA, B/CGC/15, 403 (7 June 1889)) (Fig 20).

The board offered counter-proposals but these were rejected in votes at local Liberal and Radical clubs by 160 men from day and night shifts at all three of the Company's stations (LMA, B/CGC/15, 414–16 (19 July 1889)). The board then made further concessions which were printed on large posters put up at the Company's works (one was folded and pasted into the Minute Book). The poster, entitled 'Commercial Gas Company – Stokers' Work and Time' and dated 22 July 1889 over the signature of the engineer, conceded the eight-hour shifts and 1½ days' pay on Sundays. The poster told the men that a day's work would be the operation of 72 retorts by a gang of three stokers and one barrowman. This was the lowest of the 'scales of duty' at rival gasworks. The clay for sealing would now be barrowed by 'outside labour' and the stokers' lobbies would be improved. The firemen would light nine fires a day 'clinkered only once per shift', and the scoop drivers' pay would be increased to 5s 7d a day. The poster announced: 'The above arrangements constitute a more liberal settlement, and certainly one more expensive to the Company, than the

other companies have given' (ibid, 416). The proposals were accepted (ibid, 420 (26 July 1889)), but constituted a greater victory than just the concessions made by the board, since the organised will of the Company's workers had been acknowledged. It was a reversal of the defeat of 1872. Increased wages for the carbonisers alone cost the Company an extra £7000 (LMA, B/CGC/16, np (9 October 1890)). Other wages and conditions were also improved after the 'Coal Fillers' and 'the Tippers and Truckers' also petitioned the board and the engineer had conferred with his counterparts in other companies (LMA, B/CGC/15, 428–9 (30 August 1889), 430 (6 September 1889)).

The Gas Light and Coke Company also conceded the eight hour day and extra pay for Sunday working, after negotiations with Will Thorne. The dispute also affected the position at the London docks – the moment of the gas workers' surprising victory coincided with a strike at West India Docks that soon spread, paralysing all the London docks (Cole et al 2002, 159) and becoming one of the most significant disputes in trade union history.

Of the three major gas companies, the South Metropolitan Company reimposed the 12-hour shift at the end of 1889, refusing to employ trade unionists (Cole et al 2002, 160) and bringing in a divisive profit-sharing scheme (Mills 2004, 1). As a result there was a serious and prolonged strike, and there was also a short strike at the Gas Light and Coke (Everard 1949, 279–80).

The final decade of the 19th century also saw the Commercial affected by industrial action elsewhere. A strike at collieries across County Durham, compounded by a strike of coal porters, hit coal stocks. The Company was forced to send

Fig 20 A double gang of stokers in 1899 – from left to right: J Fletcher, J A Brown, J Dean, E Jones, G Jackson, R G Knight, A Webb, A Kemp, E Southwood, J Edwards and A Webb (Co-partnership H, June 1931, 93)

a circular to consumers urging them to dispense with 'extra lights and consumption until the termination of the strike' (LMA, B/CGC/16, 234 (11 March 1892)). In later years, this period was seen as 'one of the most difficult times' for gas companies because of industrial unrest and a rise in the price of coal (LMA, B/CGC/17, np (9 April 1901)).

4.8 The Company in the 20th century, 1900–49

A profit-sharing scheme was adopted by the Company in 1901. The objects of the scheme included 'to attach the workmen to the Company, to give them a direct personal interest in its prosperity' and 'to enable the Men to improve their position in life'. Such a scheme would promote goodwill and there would be 'less danger of a strike'. The scheme was similar to those adopted by the South Metropolitan in the late 1880s and by the Crystal Palace Gas Company in 1894 (LMA, B/CGC/17, 411 (25 July 1901)).

From 1904 almost all the Company's coal was carried on its small fleet of colliers. There were eight colliers by 1918, but by 1931 only the SS *Mile End* and the SS *Stepney*, launched respectively in 1911 and 1916, were in operation (Ridge 1998, 2) (Fig 21).

During the First World War the works were adapted for munitions production. From 1915 to 1917, women were employed alongside men to make shell cases (Ridge 1998, 31).

The Company was affected by the 1926 General Strike and the board was told that the coke carmen, members of the Transport Union, 'had been forced by intimidation to cease work'. As a result the coke loaders were used as labourers at the works, although they had refused to load two vans with coke for a customer. Plans had already been laid to break any strike by gas workers. The chief engineer reported that he had 'received information through the National Gas Council that had the Trade Union Congress called out the Gas Workers, the Government would have been in a position to supply sufficient

experienced men to ensure the continuation of the Gas Supply' (LMA, B/CGC/21, 57 (13 May 1926)).

In 1931 the South Metropolitan Company became the largest shareholder in the Commercial by agreement with the board. The directors assured staff that the Company would 'retain its separate identity' (*Co-partnership H*, March 1931, 8). There was mounting concern that electricity was beginning to supersede gas, not helped by the actions of local authorities. The Company protested to the government that Stepney Borough Council was not allowing gas to be supplied to the newly built Limehouse Fields Estate, and there were fears that the replacements for 2600 recently demolished houses would also be supplied with electricity only (ibid, 31). In the mid 1930s, the chairman lamented that 'gas has been completely eliminated from the highways and by-ways of East London' (*Co-partnership H*, Christmas 1934, 246). Despite these problems, in 1934 the Company sold 17,194 lighting burners, 6763 cookers and 645 fires, with 111,673 heating appliances on rental (*Co-partnership H*, September 1935, 1). A large proportion of the Company's consumers were Jewish, and the Company benefited from increased sales at Passover as many of the households 'prefer to obtain, if it is possible, a new cooker' at this time (*Co-partnership H*, March 1931, 44).

By 1935, the directors were boasting that the Commercial sold more gas per mile of main than any other company. Its 297 miles (478km) of main served 114,950 consumers in the approximate 7 square miles (18km²) of its district. The ordinary capital of the Company was £1,770,005, of which £148,950 was held by employees to whom the Company paid £5971 weekly in salaries. As well as being a major local employer the Company made a significant contribution to the rates – 'over £33,920pa' (*Co-partnership H*, September 1935, 1).

The Wapping Works closed in 1935 as the result of a fire (*Co-partnership H*, March 1935, 5). This works had been acquired by the Commercial as part of the amalgamation with the Ratcliff in 1875. Its 2¾ acre (1.11ha) site had been built up from over 40 separate purchases of small plots of land, with portions of former buildings reused. The coal gas engine room had originally been a rice mill. The two retort houses could generate 3.25 million cubic feet (92,030m³) of gas a day by

Fig 21 Two of the Company's ships: the SS Mile End *and the SS* Stepney *(Co-partnership H, June 1931, 105)*

the 1930s. A CWG plant that could produce a further 1.25 million cubic feet (35,396m³) had gone out of use in 1927. Gas that could not be stored in the single small 220,000 cubic feet (6230m³) capacity gasholder was piped to the Stepney Works via a special main. Wapping's chief advantage was its river access, and by the 1930s it was supplying all the coal used at Stepney, delivered by a fleet of steam lorries (*Co-partnership H*, November 1931, 201–3). In 1936 the Company opened a gas-powered housing estate for its workers (Chapter 6.1 and Fig 69).

The Second World War saw the Stepney Works targeted by severe and repeated attacks, and most of the gasholders were damaged. The Company set up control rooms with engineers and other staff, including repair squads with fully equipped lorries and pneumatic paving-breakers, to deal with the results of enemy bombardment. The squads repaired mains fractured by bombs. The Company maintained gas supplies as far as possible, and was congratulated by the Regional Commissioner, Sir Warren Fisher, for the speed with which supplies were restored. The London Gas Centre provided aid from other gas companies. A fire-fighting staff was maintained at the works and men were obliged to climb up to extinguish flames from the top or sides of full gasholders damaged by bombs. Some men lost their lives while others suffered serious injuries (Lewey 1944, 32–4).

In 1944 the Ministry of Fuel and Power set up a committee of inquiry under Geoffrey Heyworth. His aim was to review the structure and organisation of the gas industry and advise what changes were necessary to develop it and reduce the price of gas to consumers. His report of December 1945 formed the basis of the Gas Act 1948 which nationalised the gas industry. Ten regional gas boards were set up in England, and one each in Scotland and Wales (Everard 1949, 366).

Faced with the prospect of nationalisation, the Commercial's board decided to follow the policy of the Gas Council and cooperate with the government's plans 'so as to ensure that the nationalized structure and organisation of the Gas Industry are such as to maintain an efficient and economic gas service to the Public' (LMA, B/CGC/23, 344 (30 May 1946)). There was an unmistakeable reluctance to relinquish the old Company, and the board recorded in its minutes that the gas industry as a whole was not necessarily in favour of the principle of nationalisation (ibid).

The Commercial was one of over 1000 separate concerns nationalised in 1949 (Stewart 1958, 44), which between them had over 3000 gasholders varying in capacity from 5000 to 12 million cubic feet (142m³ to 339,802m³) (ibid, 32). The Commercial and the Gas Light and Coke's districts were amalgamated to form the North Thames Gas Board, while the South Metropolitan along with other suburban companies became the South Eastern Gas Board (Everard 1949, 382–3).

4.9 After nationalisation

Ten years after nationalisation, there were 13 million consumers using 550,000 million cubic feet (156,000 million cubic metres) of gas a year. Half of this was for domestic use, with about 30% for industrial use, 15% for commercial use and the remainder for central government, local authorities and street lighting. The gas industry used one-eighth of the total coal mined in the country (28 million tons), and provided employment for almost 300,000 people, about half of whom were employed directly (Stewart 1958, 48).

Oil-derived feedstocks began to supplant coal for gasification from the 1950s and this in turn was superseded by natural gas from the 1970s. By 1970 the gasification of coal in London had ceased altogether. Natural gas was supplied at double the pressure, and some existing gasholders were kept in use for gas storage. These included gasholders 1–4 (**IX–XII**) at Stepney until the early 1990s, and gasholder 5 (**VIII**) until the early 1950s when it was demolished.

5

The structural development of the Stepney Works

5.1 The first structures, 1837–44

Fig 22 illustrates the development of the works, drawing on all sources of evidence – cartographic, documentary, photographic and building survey. Although the surviving minutes for the Company start in April 1844, and thus do not cover its first years, it is possible to reconstruct at least some of the earliest history of the works from later references.

Maps up to the early 19th century, for example Rocque's 1746 map (not illustrated) and Greenwood and Greenwood's 1827 map (Fig 23), show the site as undeveloped. The first gasholder tank, as well as a retort house (B1), a purifying house and a lay-by, were reputedly built about 1839 (Maddocks 1931, 24). The works almost certainly included a stores and a smithy in this phase, at least by October 1844 (LMA, B/CGC/1, 77 (30 October 1844)), together with an office (ibid, 107 (30 December 1844)); there was probably also a condenser (ibid, 352–3 (25 March 1846)) and a coal store (B2).

Three 60ft (18.29m) diameter gasholders (LMA, B/CGC/1, 495–7 (18 October 1846)), referred to at the time as gasholders 1, 2 and 3, had been erected by April 1844. These are numbered **I**, **II** and **III** for the purposes of this book. The gasholders were located along the west side of the site (LMA, B/CGC/3, 174 (12 January 1853)) and are likely to have been single-lift. They were constructed of wrought and cast iron elements, with water-filled tanks (ibid, 191 (18 February 1853)). The tanks were probably built in brick (ibid, 198 (4 March 1853)) and were probably underground, as was the case with their successors. *Cross's pocket plan of London*, published in 1847 but compiled earlier, shows only one gasholder (**I**) in addition to two rectangular buildings (Fig 24).

One of the gasholders – perhaps the third in the group to be built – may have been completed in late 1841. An advertisement by the Company in July 1841, addressed to 'Gasometer-Makers', stated that a '60-feet Gas-holder' was to be completed by 'Michaelmas-day next' (ie 29 September 1841) under penalty of £200 (*The Times*, 9 July 1841, 10).

The three early gasholders may not have been particularly high. In 1877 it was stated that for single-lift holders the typical height to diameter ratio was roughly 1:3 (Richards 1877, 201). This was broadly confirmed in a study made by Tucker of five large single-lift holder bells, in which this ratio varied between 1:2.1 and 1:4.0 (Tucker 2000, 40). The early 60ft diameter gasholders at the Stepney Works may therefore only have been about 15–30ft (4.5–9.1m) high.

5.2 Isaac Mercer's gasworks, 1844–7

The early 1840s marked a turning point for the Commercial, and towards the end of the decade – with districting agreements secured with rival companies in 1846 crowned by the achievement of the Act of Incorporation a year later – the

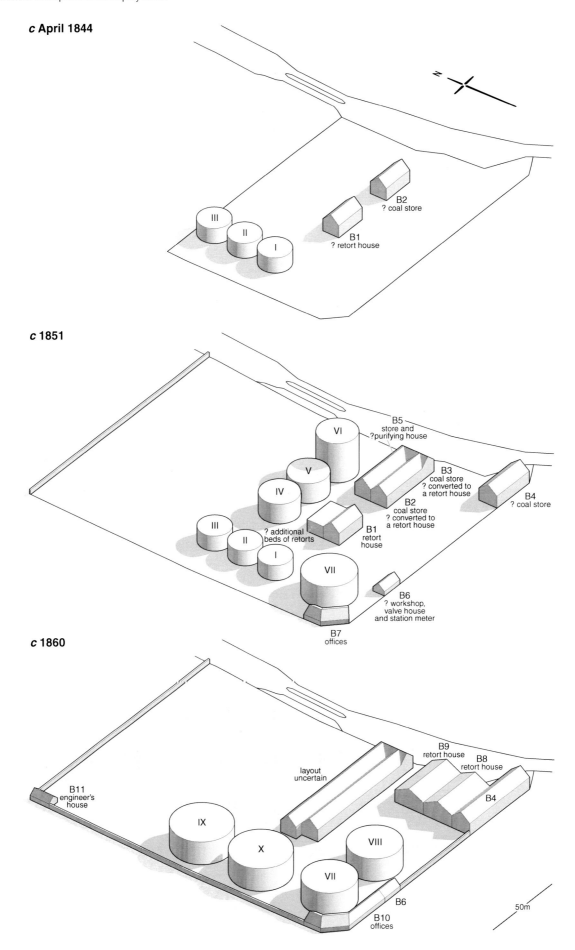

c **April 1844**

c 1851

c 1860

Fig 22 3D reconstructions showing the development of the Stepney Gasworks between c *1844 and* c *1930 (scale 1:2500)*

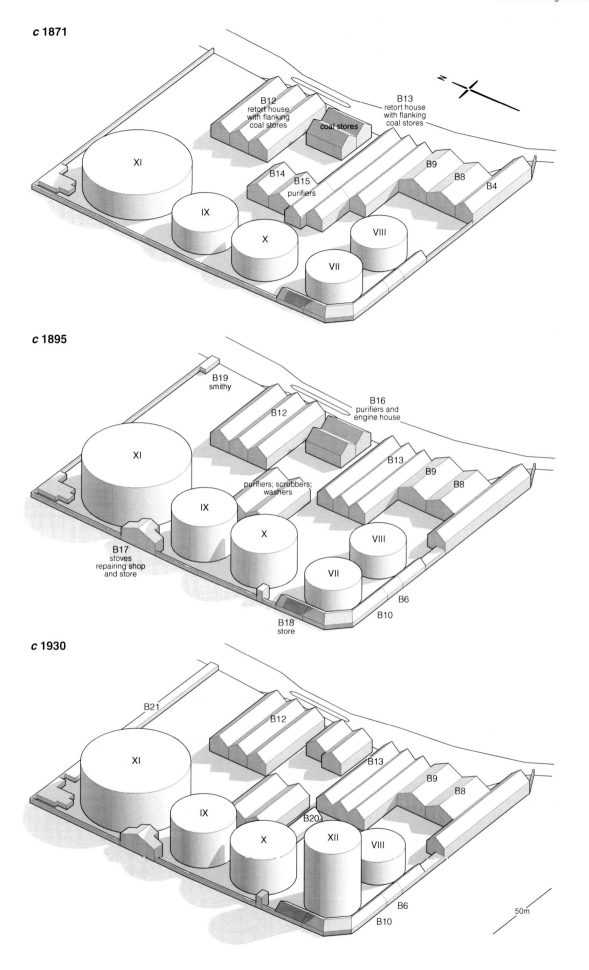

Isaac Mercer's gasworks, 1844–7

c 1871

N

B12
retort house
with flanking
coal stores

B13
retort house
with flanking
coal stores

coal stores

B14

B15
purifiers

B9

B8

B4

XI

IX

X

VIII

VII

c 1895

B19
smithy

B12

B16
purifiers and
engine house

purifiers; scrubbers;
washers

B13

B9

B8

XI

IX

X

VIII

B17
stoves
repairing shop
and store

VII

B6

B10

B18
store

c 1930

B21

B12

B13

B9

B8

XI

IX

X

B20

XII

VIII

B6

50m

B10

39

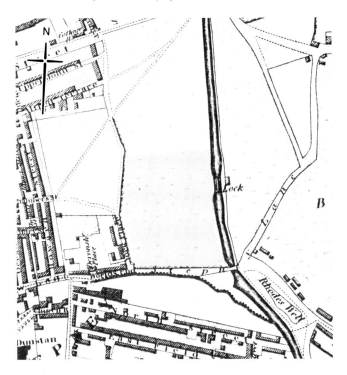

Fig 23 Detail from Greenwood and Greenwood's map of 1827 (Greenwood and Greenwood 1827)

Fig 24 Detail from Cross's plan of 1847 (Cross 1847)

Company was firmly established. The board and its engineer, Isaac Mercer, seemed undaunted by the challenge of rising demand for gas, and even though the Stepney Works was put under great strain, Mercer's improvements paid off. In 1846, the board instructed him to make two reports – in April and October – about how the works could be expanded to bring in more income. In April he told them of his plans for a new coal store and lay-by on the Regent's Canal, new gasholders, meter house, valve house, engine house, boiler house, smith's shop, storeroom and condenser. The estimated cost of £9800 would bring in an annual rental of £30,000 (LMA, B/CGC/1, 355–6 (1 April 1846)). Mercer was even more ambitious in his October report, delivered to the board in advance of a half-yearly general meeting, in which he estimated that a reduced outlay of £7000 would still secure an annual rental of £30,000–£32,000 (ibid, 495–7 (18 October 1846)). The confidence of the Company and its first engineer shines through in the Minute Books of this period.

In 1844 there was only one retort house (B1). That year, the board ordered that iron flooring be laid in it (LMA, B/CGC/1, 32 (3 July 1844)) and Mercer's October 1846 report indicated that there was only one at the works (ibid, 495–7 (18 October 1846)). It seems likely that the retort house mentioned by Mercer in 1846 was the same one as was there in 1844, since there is no mention of any demolition work between the two dates.

What is beyond doubt is that much work was done to fit out the retort house with (iron) retorts in early 1844. William Handasyde's tender of £6 5s per ton 'for Retorts' was accepted (LMA, B/CGC/1, 5 (24 April 1844)), as was Appleby Walker and Company's tender 'for the supply of 100 Retorts' at a price

of £6 3s 6d per ton (ibid, 39 (17 July 1844)). Handasyde was probably William Handyside (1793–1850), the engineer/iron founder (Skempton 2001, 15). The completed retort house contained 24 beds of retorts, with 148 retorts in total (LMA B/CGC/1, 495–7 (18 October 1846)). Mercer also drew up a specification for 'Hydraulic Mains and for the new Retort Beds' and the secretary was instructed to write to contractors for tenders (ibid, 19 (1 June 1844)). In July 1844, the board instructed that 'four benches of Retorts, 7 Retorts each be immediately fitted up in the new Ovens' (ibid, 41 (24 July 1844)), and the work began the following month (ibid, 49 (7 August 1844)). By mid 1846 there were 123 retorts, either 14in (0.35m), 20in (0.51m) or 27in (0.69m), which were charged every six hours (ibid, 385 (13 May 1846)).

In October 1846, Mercer reported that the majority of the retorts in the retort house (B1) were in action, and the rest would be operational by the end of the year. He said that the retorts lasted on average '12 to 13 months', a duration 'unprecedented in the history of retort setting', most retorts lasting only eight months. The improvement had been brought about by 'dispensing with the aid of the chimney shaft' (LMA, B/CGC/1, 495–7 (18 October 1846)), perhaps resulting in a lower draw and slower burn. When they were worn out, old retorts were sold off for scrap (ibid, 261 (12 November 1845)).

Plans to erect 'four beds of Retorts outside and against the North End of the Coal Store [B3]' were ordered to be carried out immediately in 1846 and tenders were sought for another '100 Iron Retorts' (LMA, B/CGC/1, 396 (27 May 1846)) to replace the ones that were wearing out.

Fitting out the retort house was not the only construction

work going on at Stepney. A report to the board that the coal store roof would be ready by mid July 1844 (LMA, B/CGC/1, 28 (26 June 1844)) would seem to imply that this was a new building. References to the 'Old Coal Store [B2]', distinct from this new coal store (B3) (LMA, B/CGC/2, 104 (2 June 1848)), indicate that there were two such stores in 1844.

Demand for gas was rising fast, and by March 1846 the coal store (presumably B2) was being converted into a retort house (LMA, B/CGC/1, 355–6 (1 April 1846)) and 'five additional beds of retorts' – presumably for a total of about new 30 retorts – were probably destined for this second retort house (B2) (ibid, 411 (24 June 1846)). Mercer did not refer to this conversion in his October 1846 report.

This presented a problem of where coal should be stored. Later that year the board directed that an additional coal store should be erected at the earliest possible opportunity (LMA, B/CGC/1, 437 (12 August 1846)). In September 1846 the engineer was instructed to design the new building (B4) with a capacity to store 6000 tons of coal and to apply to the Regent's Canal Company to extend the lay-by alongside it (ibid, 466 (16 September 1846)). The tender was put out in June 1847 (ibid, 603 (2 June 1847)) and the advertisement in *The Times* reveals that the new coal stores, with iron roofs, would cover 'an area of 1,200 feet' (111m^2), 'with lay-bye adjoining' (*The Times*, 9 June 1847, 2). The tender was won by John Curtis for £2497, including the roof and the lay-by (LMA, B/CGC/2, 2 (23 June 1847)), and it was further resolved that the coal store be erected on the south side of the works, harmonising with the plan for offices (ibid, 15 (11 August 1847)).

The new coal store (B4), the third to be built at the works, was still not complete in October 1847 (LMA, B/CGC/2, 38 (27 October 1847)), but was presumably finished by May 1848 when it was loaded with Pelton Main coal (ibid, 100 (19 May 1848)), kept separate from the Pelaw Main coal which was deposited in 'the Old Coal Store' (ibid, 104 (2 June 1848)). The Company was experimenting with Pelton Main coal – a 'good gas coal' – on the recommendation of the Gas Light and Coke, which had even considered purchasing Pelton Main colliery to secure its own supply some years earlier (Everard 1949, 81).

There were other storage problems too. The urgency was such that the board ordered 'an Iron Roof with slate or pantile be erected on the North side of the Retort House [presumably B2] extending from the Canal on the East side 300 feet [91.4m] and on the North side from the Retort House 200 feet [61m]' to keep the Company's stores (other than coal, presumably) under cover (B5) (LMA, B/CGC/1, 453 (2 September 1846)).

It was clear by early 1847 that extra gas-making capacity would be required, and Mercer was already drawing up plans for another 'New Retort House' (LMA, B/CGC/1, 570 (17 February 1847)) in preparation for the Company's Act of Incorporation, passed later that year. The preliminary inquiry into the Act heard that there were 180 retorts, with plans for 90 more (Maddocks 1931, 90) – presumably in the new retort house. In April 1847, the board resolved that 'the present Coal Store' (likely to be B3) should be converted into a retort house (LMA, B/CGC/1, 594 (28 April 1847)).

The board was also keen to keep up with innovations in the industry. Clay retorts had been used in conjunction with iron retorts by the Gas Light and Coke Company since 1843 (Everard 1949, 88) and would also be adopted by the South Metropolitan Company six years later, although they were not in general use until 1853 (Maddocks 1931, 172). The engineer proposed to 'build a fifth bed of Retorts at the north end of the Coal Store for the purpose of testing the Clay retorts' (LMA, B/CGC/1, 418 (1 July 1846)). In mid 1845 he asked a Mr Bethell to show him his 'apparatus for generating gas' in operation (ibid, 185–6 (15 June 1845)).

Other new buildings included a workshop for the fitters (B6) (LMA, B/CGC/1, 68 (2 October 1844)) and a 'building added to the Offices' (B7) (ibid, 107 (30 December 1844)), which was presumably the new offices ordered to be roofed in zinc (ibid, 108 (8 January 1845)). These new offices were finished about February 1845 when they were whitewashed (ibid, 118 (5 February 1845)). A staircase was planned for the lime room, indicating that this room was not on the ground floor (ibid, 606 (9 June 1847)). The lime room and boiler house – probably part of the B2/B3/B5 group of buildings – were nearly complete by August 1847, when they were being glazed (LMA, B/CGC/2, 13–14 (11 August 1847)).

The engineer's plans for a new engine house were approved in 1846 (LMA, B/CGC/1, 390 (18 May 1846)) and the building was presumably finished the following year when it was ordered to be provided with a 'zinc ceiling' (LMA, B/CGC/2, 17 (18 August 1847)). This is also likely to have been in the B2/B3/B5 group of buildings. Samuel Hodge of Limehouse won the tender to erect a steam engine for £194 (LMA, B/CGC/1, 549 (15 January 1847)) and the gearing to this was complete in mid 1847 (ibid, 608 (16 June 1847)). The engine was to be used to pump water for the retort houses and the purifying and condensing processes, as well as for supplying power for a blowing machine in the smith's shop, for a lathe and to unload coals (ibid, 495–7 (18 October 1846)). There was already a means of weighing the coal as it was delivered (ibid, 133 (12 March 1845)).

The board was also interested in developments in improving gas purity, and allowed Banks, Cormach and Company to test their method of gas purification at the works at their own expense, supervised by the engineer (LMA, B/CGC/1, 327 (18 February 1846)). The engineer was instructed to improve 'the present Condenser' and to prepare a detailed specification for a new one (ibid, 352–3 (25 March 1846)). The new condenser 'of vertical pipes of twice the size of the present one' would cost an additional £400 'exclusive of Tank for head of water which must be placed at an altitude of at least 28 feet [8.53m]' which would cost £200–£300 (ibid, 356 (1 April 1846)). This was 'a condenser on a new and improved principle' (ibid, 495–7 (18 October 1846)). Some on the board opposed the new condenser, but it was approved on a vote (ibid, 360 (8 April 1846)). Thomas Mees Bell Foundry at Brierley Hill, Birmingham, successfully tendered for 'Condenser and Tar Tank' at £695 in June 1846 (ibid, 399 (3 June 1846)), but the work was still not completed by January 1847 (ibid, 552 (22 January 1847)). Improvements were also made to the old condenser by extending the 'cooling surface in the process of condensing all Tar and Ammoniacal Vapours'. The 'old style' of condensing had resulted in the pollution of the lime in the purifiers 'in consequence of its high temperature' (ibid, 495–7 (18 October 1846)).

According to Mercer in October 1846, the 'amply capacious' purifiers were in good repair (LMA, B/CGC/1, 495–7 (18 October 1846)). However, in early 1847 the foundations to new purifiers were being laid (ibid, 569 (17 February 1847)) and G E Deeley's tender of £500 to build three wet-lime purifiers was accepted (ibid, 585 (31 March 1847)). Completion was a slow process and the purifiers were still not ready in October (LMA, B/CGC/2, 35 (3 October 1847)). The purifying house (perhaps within the B2/B3/B5 group of buildings) was being glazed in December (ibid, 56 (15 December 1847)) and the new purifiers were presumably complete by June 1848, when they required alteration (ibid, 108 (16 June 1848)).

Water was a vital component of the purification process and much else, and a deep well pump was purchased in 1844 (LMA, B/CGC/1, 53 (21 August 1844)). Nevertheless, the well could not meet all the needs of the works, as the following year the Company was using 22,000 barrels of water a year supplied by the East London Water Works Company at a cost of £40 10s (ibid, 255 (29 October 1845)). Drawing water from the adjacent canal was not an option – it was too dirty for the process, and would have required an agreement with the Regent's Canal Company.

The Company was always keen to dispose of by-products by sale, although this was not always possible. In 1844 it was estimated that the works would produce 20,000 gallons (90.9m³) of tar in the ensuing year (LMA, B/CGC/1, 48 (7 August 1844)). In 1845, 'Gas Tar' was sold to B Smith of Hackney for 1s 8d per gallon (ibid, np (4 June 1845)) and the Tyne Fuel Company bought 2000 butts of 108 gallons (491L) each for 1s 4d per gallon (ibid, 264 (19 November 1845)). Ammoniacal liquor was also sold off – in 1845, for example, Messrs Banks Crimmack bought it for 2s 6d per 108 gallons (ibid, 163 (23 April 1845)). Coke and breeze (coke dust) were sold off to merchants and others. In 1845 Maude Son and Company bought the Commercial's breeze for 7s 6d per chaldron (ibid, 220 (6 August 1845)).

In 1845, Isaac Mercer prepared the specification for an 'Oven to cleanse the foul lime' and the directors agreed that it should be erected at a cost of £50 (LMA, B/CGC/1, 144 (2 April 1845)). As for 'Refuse Lime', in 1845 a Mr Jones was authorised to dispose of it 'as he may think proper' (ibid, 169 (7 May 1845)). The Commercial was inventive in disposing of this by-product, which was often a nuisance. After offering used lime to an Essex farmer for £5 (ibid, 259 (5 November 1845)), the Company bought 100 copies of 'Johnson's Tracts on the Agricultural Use of Gas Lime etc.' to distribute to local farmers and build the market for waste lime (ibid, 260 (12 November 1845)). This ploy was not as successful as the board might have hoped, and in early 1848 refuse lime was removed from the works at a cost to the Company of £24 (LMA, B/CGC/2, 69 (26 January 1848)). It may be that the sulphur compounds in the

spent lime made it unsuitable for use as a fertiliser.

Additional gas storage capacity was also required. In early 1844, the Company advertised in *The Times* (8 April 1844, 2) for tenders to erect 'a Gasholder, of the diameter of 80 feet'. They had advertised previously for tenders to excavate and build the brickwork of the gasholder tank, but interestingly with a 'diameter of 100 feet' (ibid, 16 March 1844, 2). Presumably the size of the tank was scaled down to 80ft (24.38m) after the advertisement appeared.

Tenders for the 'new Gasholder' (**IV**) were submitted to the board in April 1844, and Deeley and Thomas's tender of £750, the lowest, was accepted (LMA, B/CGC/1, 1 (10 April 1844)). The directors wrote to Deeley eight weeks later to remind him that 'the time was drawing near for the completion of the Gasholder, and that the Tank would be ready in a fortnight's time' (ibid, 15 (29 May 1844)). In July 1844, the directors read a letter from Deeley and Thomas stating that 'the Gasholder was ready' (ibid, 32 (3 July 1844)). However, later that month the directors complained about 'the non-arrival of the Gasholder' (ibid, 42 (24 July 1844)) and again in the autumn, stating that the Commercial 'had been damaged by the delay' in its completion (ibid, 71 (9 October 1844)). Early in 1845 Deeley and Thomas requested £200, which was paid (ibid, 109 (8 January 1845)), but a further request for an 'advance' of £300 was refused until the gasholder was complete (ibid, 111 (14 January 1845)). The gasholder may finally have been finished as late as spring 1845 when a cheque for £348 1s was issued to Deeley and Thomas (ibid, 173 (14 May 1845)), although a later minute refers to the gasholder as 'erected in 1844' (ibid, 390 (18 May 1846)).

A 'Scale of feet and inches' was ordered to be marked on each of the 'Gasometers' so that the rising and falling of the bell (and so the amount of gas held) could be gauged (LMA, B/CGC/1, 181 (4 June 1845)). There seems to have been no station meter at the works at this time, and a proposal to install one was rejected (ibid, 194 (25 June 1845); 200 (9 July 1845)).

The engineer's plans for a second 80ft diameter gasholder (**V**) – 'the same size in all respects' as Deeley and Thomas's (**IV**) – were approved in 1846 (LMA, B/CGC/1, 390 (18 May 1846)). An advertisement placed in *The Times* (5 June 1846, 2) yielded a tender by Messrs Knight and Son, Limehouse for the tank of £743, which was successful (LMA, B/CGC/1, 407 (17 June 1846)). In August 1846 a cheque was issued to Messrs Knight and arrangements were made to fill 'No. 4 Gas Holder Tank' with canal water (ibid, 437 (12 August 1846)). The designation of this gasholder tank as 'No. 4' is odd, since this was the fifth gasholder at the works. One possibility is that one of the three gasholders (ie **I–III**) built before April 1844 had been pulled down and that the remaining gasholders had been renumbered. However, there is no mention of any gasholders being demolished, and in addition this does not tally with Mercer's report in 18 October 1846 (see below) in which he stated that there were five gasholders at the works.

A tender by Deeley and Thomas of £845 to build the gasholder itself was also accepted (LMA, B/CGC/1, 410 (24 June 1846)). There seem to have been problems with this tender, because only weeks later a second tender of £980 by Mr J Pope of Old Brentford, Middlesex, to complete the gasholder by October, was also initially successful (ibid, 434 (5 August 1846)); however, Pope's securities were rejected and this decision was also reversed (ibid, 437 (12 August 1846)). A third tender, by Mr Woolcott of Great Winchester Street, London, of £1000 to build the 'New Gas Holder', was accepted (ibid). The task appears to have been difficult and Woolcott requested an extension to January 1847 to complete it (ibid, 465 (16 September 1846)). The gasholder was still not finished in January, when the Minute Book records that 'Woolcott and Horton' were penalised (ibid, 549 (15 January 1847)). It was finally finished in April 1847 (ibid, 588 (14 April 1847)).

In October 1846, Mercer was able to announce to the board that 'we have three 60-feet gasholders and one 80-feet gasholder and another 80-feet gasholder in the course of erection' (LMA, B/CGC/1, 495–7, 18 October 1846). Early studies of the Company (eg Maddocks 1931, 89) assumed that only four gasholders existed at this time, because the incomplete holder was omitted from the report of the committee of inquiry prior to the Company's 1847 Act of Incorporation.

Even with five holders, storage capacity was still a problem. In spring 1847 it was resolved that 'an additional Gas Holder be ordered' (**VI**) (LMA, B/CGC/1, 587 (31 March 1847)). This was a third '80-feet diameter' holder and tank (ibid, 591 (21 April 1847)). The tenders were won by J B W Horton for erecting the gasholder for £1230 and by John Jay for building the tank for £1120 (ibid, 596 (5 May 1847)). According to an advertisement in *The Times*, the gasholder was to be 'of 80 feet diameter' and the tank '81 feet in diameter' (26 April 1847, 3). Both were complete in December and the tank was filled with canal water (LMA, B/CGC/2, 59 (22 December 1847); 64 (12 January 1848)).

The engineer was also responsible for the system of mains, at least some of which were supplied by the Butterley Iron Company (LMA, B/CGC/1, 22 (5 June 1844)). Pressure gauges were ordered to be fixed in each inspector's district so that gas pressure could be monitored (ibid, 79 (23 October 1844)). In this period, the cost of laying mains could be recouped in a few months. In 1845 Mercer estimated that by laying mains at a cost of £150 in a portion of Mile End Old Town and Bromley, a rental of about £200 per annum could be obtained (ibid, 155 (16 April 1845)).

In the first decade of its existence, Isaac Mercer was a key figure in laying the foundations of the Company's future success. However, his health had deteriorated and he retired in late 1847 with an annual pension of £150; the board praised his 'energy and perseverance' (LMA, B/CGC/2, 45 (12 November 1847)). He died just over a year later (ibid, 38 (26 January 1849)).

5.3　The beginnings of renewal, 1848–52

David Methven, formerly of Coventry Gasworks, was appointed in Mercer's place, although as superintendent rather than engineer (LMA, B/CGC/2, 50–1 (1 December 1847)). He was faced with the task of implementing his predecessor's plans which had already been agreed by the board, as well as servicing the Company's district, as defined in the Act of Incorporation. He was compelled to resign in 1850 because of his association with Alexander Croll of the Great Central Company, then a bitter rival of the Commercial (ibid, 277–8 (16 August 1850)), and was succeeded by Robert M Christie, formerly of the Phoenix Company (ibid, 305 (27 December 1850)). Methven went on to work for the Imperial Gas Company.

This phase saw no relaxation of the pace of change at the works as the Company strove to meet increasing demand for gas. In 1848 the Company paid £8490 for the freehold of all the land on which the Stepney Works stood (LMA, B/CGC/2, 141–3 (20 November 1848); LBTH, deed no. 4087, quoted in Ridge 1998, 1). The following year, a boundary wall was built along the new north boundary of the works by a Mr Tay for £10 2s 6d (LMA, B/CGC/2, 187 (7 June 1849)).

A proposal to erect a 'Valve House' in the style of the buildings at the Company's works (LMA, B/CGC/2, 102 (26 May 1848)) was agreed two weeks later, together with the provision of a station meter (ibid, 105 (9 June 1848)). Both are likely to have been additions to, or rebuildings of, B6 (first built as a workshop in 1845). Parkinson won the contract to erect the station meter for £400, including building its foundations and providing water (ibid, 113 (14 July 1848)). Stutely's tender to build the brickwork of the new meter house was accepted, as was Standing's of £70 for the roof (ibid, 143–6 (15 December 1848)). It was also decided that the valve house should have a governor (ibid, 121 (18 August 1848)). The valve and meter house was probably completed in early 1849 when it was plastered with Portland cement (ibid, 159 (9 February 1849)) and its windows glazed (ibid, 166 (2 March 1849)).

A report by the chairman, in summer 1848, ordered that a 'Building in every respect uniform with the gable end of the old Coal Store should be added to the South side of the Purifying House by this course the entire length of the buildings of Retort and Purifying House will be rendered uniform' (LMA, B/CGC/2, 109 (23 June 1848)). Other building works included an 'iron shed', built by Mr Deeley, which was completed by April 1850 (LMA, B/CGC/2, 247 (10 April 1850)), and a chimney shaft of 130ft (39.6m) height that replaced an earlier one (ibid, 341 (4 June 1851)). The tender for this latter work was won by John Jay (also building King's Cross Station and the Great Western Hotel at this time) for £909 (ibid, 349 (9 July 1851)) and the chimney shaft was completed in late 1851 (LMA, B/CGC/3, 11 (12 December 1851)).

In the retort houses the Company had been experimenting with clay retorts since at least 1846, and a committee was formally set up to consider their use in 1847 (LMA, B/CGC/1, 599 (12 May 1847)). The following year Methven was ordered to report specifically on their superior durability (LMA, B/CGC/2, 123 (1 September 1848)), a major advantage over iron. Although iron retorts still predominated (ibid, 192 (6 July 1849)), 'Foreign Clay Retorts' were ordered in 1849 (ibid, 188 (15 June 1849)). Clay retorts were being used alongside iron retorts in early 1851 (ibid, 318–19 (26 February 1851)) and at least 25 clay retorts were ordered in early 1852 (LMA, B/CGC/3, 30 (23 January 1852)). The Company seems to have switched completely to clay retorts the following year.

Innovations in purification were also being made in the gas industry, specifically the use of iron oxide. However, Superintendent Christie was 'decidedly of the opinion' that the wet lime process used by the Company with the addition of scrubbers and dry lime chambers was the best and least expensive method of purification (LMA, B/CGC/2, 339 (28 May 1851)). Christie's suggestions were adopted and the tender to erect the new purifiers, including scrubbers, was won by Mr G Brown, who intended to use both cast and wrought iron elements (ibid, 347 (25 June 1851)).

A new exhauster was required in 1848 and J and A Blyth's tender of £240 to erect this was accepted (LMA, B/CGC/2, 89 (14 April 1848)). The same company won the tender to erect a further exhauster a year later for £316 10s (ibid, 188 (15 June 1849)), and the tender for a new steam engine was won by Stewart and Wilson for £239 10s (ibid, 191 (29 June 1849)). The board decided to erect a crane in 1848 (ibid, 94 (5 May 1848)), but it is unclear whether the wrought iron crane to be erected on the Company's wharf manufactured by Walker and Jolly three years later (ibid, 344 (18 June 1851)) was the same one.

At the end of the 1840s the prospect of a steadily rising demand for gas, coupled with the 'inefficient state of two of the Gas Holders' – presumably two of the earliest – prompted the board to consider erecting another gasholder (LMA, B/CGC/2, 226–7 (2 January 1850)). However, the superintendent's assertion that the 'efficient' works could cope with the increased consumption (ibid, 246 (3 April 1850)) seems to have put the board's mind at rest, and there is no further mention of a new gasholder until late 1850. The canal water required from the Regent's Canal Company 'to fill No. 4 Gas Holder tank', presumably the one built by Knight and Son for gasholder **V**, may therefore have been needed because of a leak (ibid, 283 (11 September 1850)).

In early 1851, the board resolved that as well as telescoping the most recent gasholder (**VI**), a new gasholder should be erected of '102 x 52 feet [31.09 x 15.85m] working measure' (LMA, B/CGC/2, 315 (12 February 1851)). The new gasholder (**VII**) was to be a 'Telescope Gasholder' (*The Times*, 10 March 1851, 9), with a 30ft (9.14m) deep brick tank (LMA, B/CGC/2, 308 (8 January 1851)). The first telescopic gasholder (see Chapter 3.5) was erected at Leeds in 1826 (Stewart 1958, 33) and the first fully successful one in London was built in 1834 by the London Gas Light Company at their Vauxhall Works (Tucker 2000, 37). Gasholder **VII** was the Commercial's first purpose-built telescopic gasholder. Horton, who had built gasholder **VI** three years earlier, met the board to tell them of his 'improved system' for construction; this was rejected by the board, although he was still awarded the contract (LMA, B/CGC/2, 311 (29 January 1851)).

An article in *The Builder* later that summer revealed that the construction of the new tank (for gasholder **VII**) and other works at Stepney was almost finished. The brick tank measured 105ft (32.00m) diameter and 32ft (9.75m) deep, and was surrounded by a 'made puddle 2 feet 6 inches [0.76m] in width'. The walls were set in blue lias lime mortar with some 'Roman cement', both of which were hydraulic (capable of setting under water). The gasholder was also equipped with a 32ft deep brick well with inlet and outlet pipes, connected to the tank by a short tunnel. The tank wall had 12 counterforts (buttresses), each topped with a Bramley Fall stone into which a 52ft (15.85m) high cast iron hollow column was bolted to form the superstructure of the gasholder (*The Builder* 1851). The tank was built by Messrs Knight (LMA, B/CGC/2, 344 (18 June 1851)) and completed by October 1851 when the Company considered the question of filling it with canal water (ibid, 367 (10 October 1851)); subsequently it must have done so, although it had still had not paid the bill to the Regent's Canal Company 'for filling No. 7 Gas-holder Tank with water' by December (LMA, B/CGC/3, 11 (12 December 1851)). The completion of the gasholder itself was considerably delayed. The board was frustrated that iron work for the 'New Gas-holder' was not delivered promptly to the Stepney Works (LMA, B/CGC/2, 342 (11 June 1851)) and when 'stay rods' finally appeared, they were found not to be to the required specification (ibid, 348 (25 June 1851)). Eventually, the Company had to contact its solicitor about the matter (ibid, 359 (5 September 1851)). Gasholder **VII** was finally certified as finished in December 1851 (ibid, 11 (12 December 1851)).

The lifts to gasholder **VII** were 102ft (31.09m) in diameter on the lower lift and 100ft (30.48m) on the upper lift, both being 26ft (7.92m) high. The capacity was 416,000 cubic feet (11,779m^3) and the pressure 5inH$_2$O (1245N/m^2) (Colburn 1865, 82).

With the completion of the second Horton gasholder (**VII**), there were now seven gasholders on the site in total. The reference to gasholder **VII** being completed in 1850 (Colburn 1865, 82) is mistaken.

5.4   Reconstruction, 1852–9

This period of development includes the earliest surviving structural remains identified by the MOLA survey. In this section an overview of the period based on historical and cartographic sources is followed by descriptions of the main surveyed structures.

Documentary and cartographic evidence

The year 1852 marked the beginning of the most comprehensive modernisation of the works that the Company had seen. At the start of the year, the board discussed extending the works so that 12 million cubic feet (3.4 million cubic metres) of gas a week could be generated (LMA, B/CGC/3, np (13 February 1852)). The directors were buoyed by the retreat of the rival British Company from London, but were also aware that they were in danger of failing to meet the rising demand for gas. The pace of remodelling the works accelerated in 1853 after a special meeting of the board decided to invest £50,000 – a huge sum for the time (and equivalent to several million pounds in current terms) – in the plans (ibid, 170 (5 January 1853)). The Company was not the only London concern modernising its works at this time. The Gas Light and Coke was also expanding its Westminster and Brick Lane Works in the 1850s (Everard 1949, 192), as were many others.

The board's plans were ambitious, although they were constrained by the freehold for the north part of the works, which specified what could be built within 150 yards (137m) of the northern boundary (LMA, B/CGC/3, 177 (14 January 1853)). A new retort house was built, the earliest three gasholders were replaced with three new ones, and a new purification plant was installed.

The entries in the Minute Books for 1853 convey the urgency to complete the expansion of the Stepney Works. There was frustration with the slow progress, combined with fear of escalating demand. Not only had the Company inherited the former consumers of the British, but the increasing price of tallow and oil was encouraging consumers to switch to gaslight (Maddocks 1931, 223). On top of this, the metropolis was expanding – the Company was now installing gas supplies into houses under construction (LMA, B/CGC/2, 371 (24 October 1851)). As a stopgap, between October and December 1853 it was compelled to undertake carbonising at the works at Schoolhouse Lane, Ratcliff, acquired from the British Company the previous year (LMA, B/CGC/3, 299 (14 October 1853); 327 (23 December 1853)).

The 1853 remodelling of the works coincided with trials of iron oxide to purify the gas, in addition to wet and dry lime. The Company was also reputedly the first in London to switch completely from iron to clay retorts (Colburn 1865, iv), apparently in early 1853. As the Company abandoned the use of iron there was a sharp increase in the number of clay retorts ordered: 50 were ordered from three firms in early 1852 (LMA, B/CGC/3, 45 (27 February 1852)), and although iron retorts were still being used in late 1852 (ibid, 114 (10 September 1852)), a huge order for 252 clay retorts was placed in early 1853 (ibid, 174 (12 January 1853)). Most of these must have been intended for the new retort house (B8) that the board had decided should be 'erected immediately' the previous autumn (ibid, 117 (17 September 1852)), and the remainder for the other retort houses at the works. The superintendent was also ordered to make plans for 'the further extension of the Retort House Coal Store &c' (ibid, 148 (26 November 1852)), presumably an extension to the west end of B4. The brickwork for the new retort house was built by Messrs Knight (ibid, 153 (3 December 1852)) and the tender for the roof was won by Standing (ibid, 121 (24 September 1852)). Standing was paid £200 and Knight £350 early the next year (ibid, 176 (14 January 1853)) with further payments made in March and April 1853 (ibid, 197 (4 March 1853); 211 (1 April 1853)) when the roof was complete (ibid, 229 (29 April 1853)). The board resolved to install ten additional beds of retorts in the 'New Retort House'

and extend 'the present New Retort House' (B8) with coal stores (ibid, 221 (15 April 1853)).

The reconstruction of the works also extended to other buildings. It was resolved that 'New Offices [B10] be erected on the South West corner of the Company's Works', with a basement storeroom (LMA, B/CGC/3, 223 (15 April 1853)). The 'Old Offices' (B7) were torn down for £85 (ibid, 294 (7 October 1853)). Mr Perry was contracted to erect 'Walls to Extension of Retort House [presumably B9], Engine and Boiler House, General Stores, meter and Governor House and Offices of the Company [B10]' for £6897 (ibid, 239 (20 May 1853)).

The board decided that there should be a 'New Entrance to the Company's Works' (LMA, B/CGC/3, 286 (16 September 1853)) and that the boundary wall on the south side of the works should be completed (ibid, 383 (28 April 1854)). A dwarf brick wall and new timber fence replaced an old dilapidated fence along the canal (ibid, 218 (8 April 1853); 247 (10 June 1853)).

Competing pressures on space at the Stepney Works between coal storage, carbonising and gas storage had to be balanced by the board and the engineer. In May 1853 the board resolved to remove beds of burnt-out retorts in 'the New Coal Store' to make room for 10,000 tons of coal (LMA, B/CGC/3, 241 (27 May 1853)), 50,000 tons having been ordered for the next 12 months (ibid, 235 (13 May 1853)).

Messrs Burton were engaged to erect the iron roof to the 'Retort House and Coal Store' for £850 (LMA, B/CGC/3, 242 (27 May 1853)). Messrs Furnival were paid £159 9s 10d for slating the 'Roof of the New Retort House' (ibid, 258 (8 July 1853)). Robert Christie, the superintendent, was ordered to report 'when the roof over the New Retort House and Coal Store, will be erected' (ibid, 305 (4 November 1853)). The Horseley Company won a tender for the roof of the engine and boiler house for £286, for the 'Condenser supply box' for £1156 and for 'Connecting Mains &c' for £1047 (ibid, 227 (22 April 1853)).

Although he had pioneered the change to clay retorts, the upheaval of rebuilding the works proved too much for Robert Christie, whose letter of resignation as superintendent on 28 February 1854 cited 'difficulties in finishing the Works now in hand' as well as 'a want of confidence of certain members of your Board' (LMA, B/CGC/3, 389 (5 May 1854)). The board's faith in him may have been shaken by the fact that it took two years to construct the first of the new gasholders (**VIII**, below). Christie went on to direct the building of the Crystal Palace District Gasworks (Colburn 1865, 44). He was succeeded at the Commercial by Robert Jones (1812–95), manager of the Wolverhampton Gas Company since 1848, who told the board he wanted to 'break a lance' with the London gas makers. Jones was to serve 26 years as one of the Company's most successful engineers and thereafter as a director. He was described as 'short-tempered and of a restless disposition' by his former boss, but energetic and with good business habits (LMA, B/CGC/3, 393 (5 May 1854)).

Increased generation of gas meant more by-products: 1000 chaldrons of coke were sold to the East London Water

Company in early 1855 (LMA, B/CGC/3, 507 (5 January 1855)). The expansion of the works required new purification plant. Two sets of wet lime purifiers were to be built, in addition to vertical condensers with 'a jet of water playing on them' (LMA, B/CGC/3, 196 (28 February 1853)). Messrs Melrose won the tender for the new purifiers and ironwork for £2996 (ibid, 242 (27 May 1853)). These were still not finished by October 1853 (ibid, 299 (14 October 1853)), but were almost certainly completed by 1855 (ibid, 540 (16 March 1855)). It was also resolved to use covered tanks for the refuse lime and lime water (ibid, 205 (18 March 1853)).

Frank Clarke Hills of Deptford had written to the board concerning his 'method of Purification of Gas by Oxide of Iron' in 1851 (LMA, B/CGC/2, 353 (30 July 1851)). He had been experimenting with this method of purification since 1849 (Trueman 1997, 15). However, it was not until 1853 that he was allowed to trial his system at the works (LMA, B/CGC/3, 310 (11 November 1853)). This was not a success initially, and complaints from customers about the quality of the gas compelled the Company to switch back to wet and dry lime purification (ibid, 325 (16 December 1853)). Hills complained that his system had been used satisfactorily at other works (ibid, 326 (23 December 1853)). Iron oxide was generally adopted for purification by 1853, especially with revivication (Stewart 1958, 24): this process, patented by Hills, involved exposing the spent oxide to air, allowing oxygen to react with the iron sulphide, releasing sulphur and reforming iron oxide (Trueman 1997, 15) which could then be reused.

Robert Jones, the Commercial's new engineer, proposed altering the mechanics of the purification process by passing the gas through two sets of purifiers at once rather than passing it through consecutive purifiers. This, he claimed, would reduce blue billy. He also proposed redirecting the foul gases back into the flues of the retort beds to decompose them. He required two new purifiers and suggested replacing the 'Brick Building over the present Wet Lime Purifiers' with an iron roof supported on iron columns on an iron floor. Oxide could then be spread on the roof for revivification (LMA, B/CGC/3, 540 (16 March 1855)), although some were sceptical of the success of such a method (Clegg 1866, 392).

It was clear by the end of 1856 that an increase in purifying power was still required (LMA, B/CGC/4, 4 (4 December 1856)) and a few months later the board approved Jones's plans to remove the condenser and build new scrubbers at a cost of £900 (ibid, 28 (1 May 1857)). A Mr Edie's tender of £8 5s per ton for a new condenser and scrubber was accepted later that year (ibid, 63 (23 October 1857)).

The expansion of the works required new machinery, and it was agreed that two 'new Engines of 20 horsepower' would be provided and a new engine house built. An additional exhauster was to be provided together with an additional station meter, capable of passing 70,000 cubic feet (1982m³) of gas per hour, and a tar tank, to be constructed out of reused iron plates (LMA, B/CGC/3, 195 (28 February 1853)). The tender for the two engines, boiler and exhauster was won by Messrs Burton for £1680 and the tender for the station meter and governor by

Parkinson for £670 (ibid, 208–9 (28 March 1853)). Burton's work seems to have been complete by September when he received a staged payment (ibid, 290 (30 September 1853)), although the firm went bankrupt the following year (ibid, 379 (21 April 1854)).

Later, an engineer's house (probably B11) was built by Lemon for £100 (LMA, B/CGC/4, 2 (28 November 1856)) and a 'Stokers' lobby and dining room' erected for £210 (ibid, 167 (24 June 1859); 169 (8 July 1859)). The engineer prepared a specification for 'a Coke Ground', and the tender to build this was also won by Lemon (ibid, 183 (30 September 1859)). The coke ground probably lay to the west of retort houses B8 and B9.

Even with seven holders, gas storage was still an issue. The board considered erecting a further gasholder in early 1852 (LMA, B/CGC/3, 29 (23 January 1852)). This 'Telescope Gasholder' (**VIII**) was to be 102ft (31.09m) in diameter, and the 104ft (31.70m) diameter tank was to be built in brick (*The Times*, 4 March 1852, 2). The tender for erecting this gasholder was won by Standing for £2956, and for the tank by John Jay for £1971 initially (LMA, B/CGC/3, 52–3 (12 March 1852)), although a further round of tendering saw the success of Knight and Son's tender of £1718 to build the tank (ibid, 55 (19 March 1852)). The 1852 date given by Colburn (1865, 82) presumably refers to the date the work was commissioned, since there were severe delays in completing both tank and gasholder. The tank was probably completed in 1853 when a payment was made to Knight (LMA, B/CGC/3, 190 (14 February 1853)), who requested the balance for the gasholder tank in June, although it had not been certified by the superintendent at this time (ibid, 244 (3 June 1853)).

In April 1853 the board contacted its solicitor 'to ensure the speedy completion of Standing's contract' (LMA, B/CGC/3, 227 (22 April 1853)), but by September Standing's gasholder (**VIII**) was still not ready (ibid, 278 (2 September 1853)). There seem to have been significant problems with its construction. The superintendent was ordered to report on the condition of the gasholder 'being erected by Mr Standing' in early 1854 (ibid, 350 (17 February 1854)). Progress must have halted, because Standing was told to 'resume the Work as soon as possible' (ibid, 353 (24 February 1854)); he responded that he would call in 'a competent Person' at his own expense to give his opinion on the state of the gasholder (ibid, 361 (10 March 1854)). Standing asked for the payment of the balance in May 1854 (ibid, 395 (12 May 1854)), suggesting that he considered the gasholder complete, although the account had still not been settled in early 1855 (ibid, 525 (16 February 1855)).

The lifts of this 416,000 cubic feet (11,779m³) capacity gasholder were both 26ft (7.92m) high, with the lower lift 102ft (31.09m) in diameter and the upper 100ft (30.48m). The pressure was 5inH₂O (1245N/m²) (Colburn 1865, 82). In May 1853 the board made an application to the East London Water Works for a supply of water to fill 'No. 1 Gasholder' (LMA, B/CGC/3, 235 (13 May 1853)) and a fee of £100 was agreed (ibid, 252 (24 June 1853)), although it is not clear whether this refers to the old gasholder (**I**) or the new one (**VIII**).

The surveyed structures

Perimeter structures

At the time of the MOLA survey the perimeter wall incorporated the remains of several gasworks buildings (eg Fig 25). The wall of the coal store along Ben Jonson Road (then Rhodeswell Road) is shown on the 1870 Ordnance Survey map (see below, Fig 42) as having ten recessed bays and 11 pilasters. The MOLA survey showed that the recess in each bay was 2.38m (7ft 10in) wide and each pilaster 1.83m (6ft) wide overall (Fig 26). The pilasters widened towards the wall face. The wall was two and a half bricks thick, or 0.60m (2ft). The 1891 Goad plan (see below, Fig 50) described the coal store as three storeys high, but the surviving stretch of wall survived to an average height of 3.5m (11ft 6in) above external pavement level. The coal store walls would have had to withstand considerable loads. There is evidence of this in the form of the cast iron wall plates, which would have held horizontal ties extending through the coal store to counteract the weight of materials stored inside it tending to push the walls outwards.

Further west, the wall was of similar construction, although the recessed bays were wider at 3.26m (10ft 8in) wide and the pilasters narrower at 1.07m (3ft 6in) (Fig 27). At the truncated top of the wall was a brick cornice that broke over the pilasters, probably representing a string course at the level of the former first floor. There was no sign of wall plates here, and

each bay had a small blocked-up arched window measuring 0.47m (1ft 6in) wide.

The bays in the south wall of the meter house (identified with reference to the Goad plan, Fig 50) were 2.89m (9ft 6in) wide and the pilasters 1.28m (4ft 2in) wide (Fig 28). Each bay was pierced with window openings, subsequently blocked, the lower windows lighting a basement. The wall was one brick thick, with a small circular cast iron wall-tie plate visible within each bay. A stub of masonry on the inside face of the wall was the remains of a floor, 1.69m (5ft 6in) above external pavement level.

Immediately west of the meter house, the walls to the 'workshops' (although all the buildings between the coal store and the offices, including the meter house, are labelled 'workshops' on the 1870 Ordnance Survey map; see Fig 42) were 0.27m (11in) thick. As with the meter house, the pilasters were 1.28m (4ft 2in) wide and the recesses of the bays 2.89m (9ft 6in) wide (Fig 29). This section of wall also incorporated basement and ground floor windows, now infilled, which were all without frames. The cross section showed that the internal ground floor level was at 9.95m (32ft 8in) OD or 2.15m (7ft) above external pavement level. In each bay the heads of the lower windows were represented by two small adjoining segmental arches, the eastern of which extended into a pilaster. Although this may imply some alteration (ie that the pilasters were added features), the pilasters were integral to the whole wall. This suggests the windows were added to suit the layout

Fig 25 View north along Harford Street showing the perimeter wall incorporating the external elevation of the Company office (to the right) and other buildings

Fig 26 Orthogonal view looking north, showing the remains of the external face of the coal store (east end) fronting on to Ben Jonson Road

Fig 27 Orthogonal view looking north, showing the remains of the external face of the coal store (west end) fronting on to Ben Jonson Road

of the building, piercing the wall at an inappropriate spot. They may have been added to allow access for services.

Further west, the walls to the Company's two-storey offices bore a greater degree of decoration: the recessed bays were narrower than elsewhere, with Portland stone string courses beneath projecting brickwork; the bottom of the Portland stone was defined by a projecting courses of tile (Fig 30; Fig 31). This building was the Company's public face (cf Fig 3), constructed in 1853 and replacing an earlier structure, or incorporating it in an altered form. The wall here was 0.23m (9in) thick, the pilasters 0.65m (2ft 2in) wide and the recessed bays 1.62m (5ft 4in) wide. This section included now infilled

Fig 28 Orthogonal view looking north, showing the remains of the external face of the meter house fronting on to Ben Jonson Road

Fig 29 Orthogonal view looking north, showing the remains of the external face of the 'workshop' fronting on to Ben Jonson Road

ground floor windows with sandstone sills at the centre of each bay. The internal ground floor level here was marked by a cut-off stub of masonry on the inside face of the wall, 1.71m (5ft 7in) above external pavement level.

The entrance front of the offices faced obliquely on to Harford Street and Ben Jonson Road, drawing attention from both streets with its relatively lavish stuccoed decoration. All that remained of the building was a truncated segment of its front wall with an infilled doorway and windows. Either side of the door were two recessed bays, each pair defined by channelled, stuccoed pilasters. The pilasters were 0.66m (2ft 2in) wide and the bays 1.57m (5ft 2in) wide. A chamfered plinth

Fig 30 Orthogonal view looking north-east, showing the remains of the external face of the head office fronting on to the junction of Ben Jonson Road and Harford Street

Fig 31 Orthogonal view looking north, showing the remains of the external face of the head office fronting on to Ben Jonson Road

with a double-stepped profile extended downwards from 9.04m (29ft 8in) OD, breaking forward to encompass the pilasters.

A blocked window opening occupied the centre of each bay. Below each window was a rectangular plastered apron surrounded by bolection moulding. Two corbels beneath each windowsill were decorated with Doric guttae. The contiguous wall to the north of the office frontage shared its decorative elements.

Fig 32 View looking south-east, showing the infilled former site entrance on Harford Street (1m scale)

Fig 33 Orthogonal view looking north-west, showing the gas lamp standard on the northern flanking pier of the former site entrance

The entrance to the works was located north of the offices on Harford Street, defined by a pair of square, brick-built piers. By the time of the survey, the entrance was blocked, although unlike the other walls it survived to its full height of 4.3m (14ft 1in) above external pavement level. Each pillar bore a shallow rectangular recess and was crowned with a Tuscan-style capital (Fig 32). Set upon each capital was a cast iron gas lamp shaft, with a barley-twist decoration (Fig 33).

Gasholders IX and X

By 1852 the early gasholders – built the best part of a decade or more earlier – were showing their age, and the superintendent was ordered to report on 'the Cost of repairing No. 1 Gas-holder' (presumably gasholder **I**) (LMA, B/CGC/3, 95 (23 July 1852)). But by the beginning of 1853 the board had decided 'to have two Gas-holders [**IX** and **X**] Erected on the Ground occupied at present by Nos 1, 2 and 3 Gas-holders [**I–III**]' along the west side of the works (ibid, 174 (12 January 1853)). An advertisement in *The Times* reveals that the gasholders were

both to be telescopic and the tanks each 125ft (38.1m) in diameter (16 February 1853, 1). The tender for demolition of the old gasholders was won by Charles Walker and Sons, who paid the Company for the scrap wrought and cast iron (LMA, B/CGC/3, 191 (18 February 1853)). The Horseley Company won the tender to build the two new gasholders (**IX** and **X**) for £10,750 and John Jay won the tender to build the two tanks for £6137 (ibid, 198 (4 March 1853)). The gasholders may have been finished in 1853 (Colburn 1865, 82). They were certainly complete by spring 1854, when Horseley received a large payment (LMA, B/CGC/3, 367 (24 March 1854)), apparently ahead of the delayed gasholder **VIII**. Staged payments were made to Jay in 1853 (ibid, 229 (29 April 1853); 244 (3 June 1853)) and he asked for the balance 'for Building Gas-holder Tanks' in March the following year (ibid, 363 (17 March 1854)), a payment of £1400 being made in May 1854 (ibid, 400 (26 May 1854)). This presumably indicates that the tanks were also finished, although Jay promised to fix a leak later that year (ibid, 491 (24 November 1854)).

The two new gasholders each had brick tanks and two lifts,

the lower lift 122ft (37.19m) in diameter and 24ft 6in (7.47m) high, and the upper lift 119ft 4in (36.37m) in diameter and 26ft (7.92m) high (Fig 34 shows gasholder **IX** after modifications in 1892). The capacity of each was 580,000 cubic feet (16,423m^3), with the pressure equal to 3^1/$_2$inH$_2$O (872N/m^2). The holders were described as having flat, untrussed crowns (Colburn 1865, 82).

Gasholders **IX** and **X** (numbered 2 and 3 respectively after 1864) were recorded during the MOLA survey. Only the survey results for the original fabric of the gasholders are described here, with details of modifications described in later sections. One major modification was the heightening of both gasholders in 1892. As might be expected, the twin gasholders shared features, dimensions and overall style. Both were early examples of a 'giant single-order, single-tier' guide frame, Type 11 in Tucker's classification (Tucker 2000, 29). This design of free-standing columns linked only at the top by girders required large column bases for stability.

Both gasholders were circular column-guided structures, 53ft 4in (16.26m) high when completed in 1854. The hollow cast iron columns were bolted together in several sections by internally flanged butt joints, so keeping the castings to a manageable size and weight. Originally each column would have consisted of three sections, as two of the five sections recorded during the survey were inserted in 1892 (NGA, NT, COG/E/P/1). The columns of this sort of guide frame were almost always styled in the Tuscan order, based on classical precedents in masonry, although of slimmer proportions (Tucker 2000, 45, 51). Such classical models only began to fall out of favour in the following decade, when they were seen as inappropriate from both mechanical and aesthetic standpoints. Tapered cast iron standards began to be used instead (ibid, 51–2). The 14 columns, which tapered with height, were 8.77m (28ft 9in) apart, measured from centre to centre. The very large

toroidal bases concealed holding-down bolts on the cast iron plinths, which were set on to stone foundations. Each base was 1.64m (5ft 5in) in diameter at its widest. The bases would originally have been complemented by Tuscan capitals, since lost, at the top of the columns (ibid, 29). The guide posts on the inner sides of the columns were still present, extending the full height of the columns in gasholder 2 (**IX**) and two-thirds of the height of the columns in gasholder 3 (**X**). Parts of the guide frame of gasholder 2 were salvaged during demolition in 2003 and have been used as historical features within new development (below, 5.8).

Both gasholders had circular substructural tanks with internal diameters of 38.16m (125ft 2in) (Figs 35–38). The depth of the tank to gasholder 2 (**IX**) was 8.29m (27ft 2in) deep and to gasholder 3 (**X**) 8.08m (26ft 6in) deep. The tanks were lined with brickwork in regular courses in a mixture of English bond and English Garden Wall bond. The dumpling in the tank of gasholder 2 (**IX**) was 7.06m (25ft 2in) above the base of the tank, and the dumpling of gasholder 3 was 6.85m (22ft 6in) above the base of the tank. There were traces of Roman (ie hydraulic) cement render surviving on the interior of the tanks and forming the surface of the dumplings.

The days of the other older gasholders were coming to an end. In 1857 the board accepted the engineer's proposal 'as regards the removal of the small Gasholders and converting the Tanks of the same into Liquor and Tar Tanks' (LMA, B/CGC/4, 28 (1 May 1857)). The gasholders in question were almost certainly two or all of Deeley and Thomas's 1845 gasholder (**IV**), Woolcott's 1847 gasholder (**V**) and Horton's 1848 gasholder (**VI**). The two circular tar wells shown on the Goad map of 1891 (see below, Fig 50) mark the former position of two gasholders, and an entry in the Minute Books confirms this. The remodelling of the works in the 1850s (Fig 39), of

*Fig 34 Gasholder 2 (**IX**) looking north-west*

which the demolition of these gasholders was a part, represented a reorganisation into a more logical arrangement where the position of structures reflected their place in the chain of processes taking place. Now coal was delivered, stored and carbonised in the east part of the works; the resulting gas was purified in the central part and stored in gasholders in the west part.

In 1857 major repairs were made to gasholder tanks using 30,000 bricks bought for this purpose (LMA, B/CGC/4, 33

(22 May 1857); 34 (29 May 1857)) and the board approved the engineer's proposed alterations and repairs to 'Gasholders No. 1 and 2' (ibid, 68 (20 November 1857)). The demolition of the pre-1850 gasholders had evidently necessitated a change in the way the Company numbered the remaining holders. Subsequent entries in the Minute Books reveal that what they referred to as 'Gasholder 1' was probably **VII** and that 'Gasholder 2' was almost certainly **VIII**. The engineer was instructed to discuss the proposed alterations with Benjamin

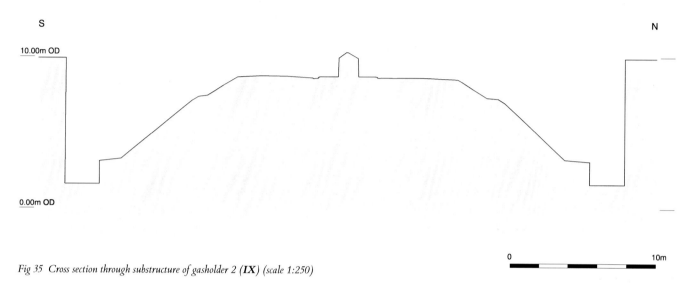

Fig 35 Cross section through substructure of gasholder 2 (**IX**) (scale 1:250)

Fig 36 View looking north across the dumpling of gasholder 2 (**IX**)

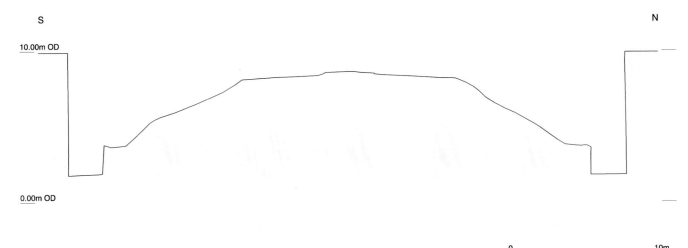

S

N

10.00m OD

0.00m OD

*Fig 37 Cross section through substructure of gasholder 3 (**X**) (scale 1:250)*

0   10m

*Fig 38 View looking north-west across the dumpling of gasholder 3 (**X**)*

Whitehouse (ibid, 72 (11 December 1857)), who was paid the balance of his account for his work on 'No. 1 Gasholder' the following year (ibid, 123 (17 September 1858)). After this, the board approved Whitehouse to undertake repairs to 'Standing's Gasholder' (**VIII**) (ibid, 130 (29 October 1858)) and his tender of £795 for this work was accepted (ibid, 133 (19 November 1858)), the repairs being completed by the following summer (ibid, 169 (8 July 1859)).

5.5 Expansion, 1860–74

Documentary and cartographic evidence

The Minute Books in this period convey the impression of a mature, well-established and confident company in control of its affairs. Output was increasing, although it was still a strain to

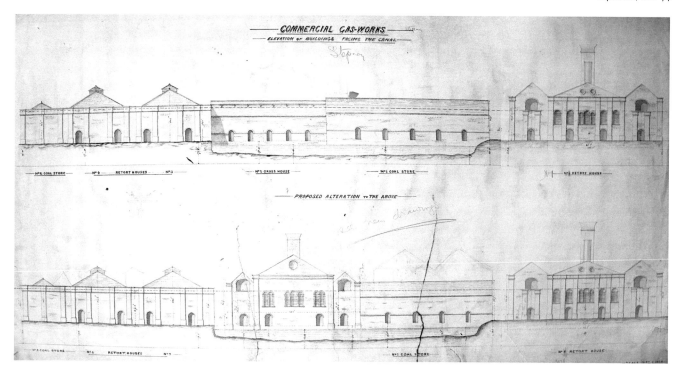

Fig 39 Elevation of buildings facing the canal in c 1870 (NGA, NT, COG/E/A/1)

keep pace with demand. The 1860 Metropolis Gas Act not only secured the Company exclusive rights of supply to its district, but also demonstrated that when the metropolis's gas companies acted together they could influence the outcome of legislation in their favour. This cooperation was useful in other ways, for example in controlling the gas companies' workers, who were becoming increasingly unionised. Cooperation helped break the 1872 strike, although it would have been an uncomfortable lesson for the boards of the metropolitan companies in the power of gas workers to shut down the industry. There were other clouds on the horizon. This period saw a major up-scaling both of works (the Gas Light and Coke's Beckton and the Imperial's Bromley Works) and of gas companies themselves (with the amalgamations of the 1870s). With the construction of its Poplar Works and its amalgamation with the Ratcliff, the Commercial replicated these changes in miniature.

Three important maps of London, published in the late 1850s to early 1870s, show the development of the Stepney Works in this period. Weller's *Postal map of London*, published in 1858 (Fig 40), shows four gasholders (**VII–X**), the southern pair smaller than the northern, as well as two substantial L-shaped buildings, set well back from the Regent's Canal which forms the eastern boundary to the works. Rhodes Well Road and York Place form the southern and western boundaries (modern Ben Jonson Road and Harford Street respectively). Weller's map also shows a boundary separating the works buildings from open land to the north, although this open land had been purchased by the Company a decade before Weller's map was published. Weller also omits Johnson's Lock on Regent's Canal, suggesting that the map may be unreliable in its detail. Other buildings at the works are depicted in the south-west and south-east corners.

Stanford published a map of the area in 1862 (Fig 41), although it was probably surveyed in the mid 1850s. The map shows the 'Commercial Gas Works' consisting of four

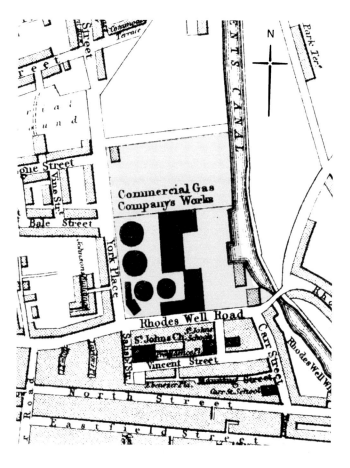

Fig 40 Detail from Weller's Postal map of London of 1858 (Weller 1858)

gasholders, with the two southern gasholders slightly smaller than the northern pair; a substantial set of buildings adjacent to the canal; and a smaller set of buildings at the junction of Rhodeswell Road and Cologne Street (formerly York Place). Like Weller, Stanford depicts the northern part of the site as empty apart from an isolated building in the north-west corner.

It is difficult to reconcile the buildings depicted by Weller in 1858 with those shown in Stanford's map published only a few years later. If Weller's map is correct, then there was a significant amount of demolition at the works between its compilation and Stanford's.

Although there are differences of size, the four gasholders (VII–X) feature on both maps. Buildings along the east side of York Place/Cologne Street are also depicted, albeit with some differences – for example the building in the south-west corner of the works is shown at an angle by Weller, but parallel to the street by Stanford; a building to the south-west of gasholder X is shown by Stanford, but not by Weller; and the southern half of the building shown in the north-west corner of the works by Weller seems to have been demolished before Stanford compiled his map.

However, it is the difference between the depiction of buildings in the central and eastern part of the works that is most striking. At the very least, substantial buildings shown by Weller immediately east of gasholder 2 (IX) and immediately east of gasholder 5 (VIII) were gone by the time Stanford compiled his map, and buildings immediately north and south of gasholder 5 (VIII) shown by Weller survived at best in only modified form in 1862. Stanford shows a new range of buildings fronting on to the canal, apparently incorporating a building in the south-east corner of the works shown by Weller, while a second building here seems to have been demolished to create a larger wharf area.

It seems likely that Weller's map was compiled while the works was being significantly remodelled. As has been noted above, at least two – and probably all – of the three remaining pre-1850 gasholders (IV, V and VI) were demolished in 1857. These were located near the canal, and this explains the curiously empty space between the buildings depicted by Weller and the canal, since this was the space that the gasholders formerly occupied.

There are also marked differences between Stanford's map and the more detailed Ordnance Survey map published in 1870 (Fig 42), although the differences are more clearly the result of the development of the works. As well as the four gasholders depicted by Stanford, the Ordnance Survey map shows the new gasholder 1 (XI), built in 1864, in the north-west corner of the site. Each pair of gasholders – labelled 'Gasometers' – shares a well, apart from gasholder 1, which was provided with its own well.

The substantial buildings depicted by Stanford in the eastern part of the site are labelled in the 1870 Ordnance Survey map as a retort house – apparently an L shape – with a north–south aligned coal store to the north, also fronting directly on to the canal, and a second coal store, aligned east–west, to the south, where there is a canalside wharf and crane. The central part of the works is occupied by an engine house and two purifying houses. The five unlabelled circular structures just north of the engine house are probably scrubbers, and the square structure just north of those is probably a washer. The northern purifying house does not appear to feature on the Stanford map, and thus had presumably been added by 1870. Another addition is an east–west aligned retort house, flanked on each long side by a coal store, near Johnson's Lock.

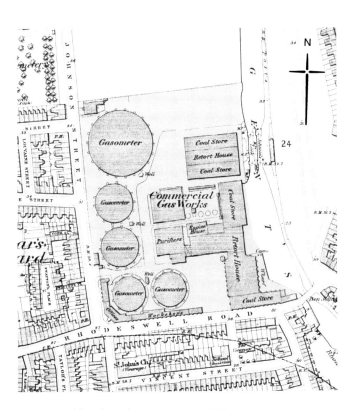

Fig 41 *Detail from Stanford's 'Library Map', 1862 (Stanford 1862)*

Fig 42 *Detail from the Ordnance Survey map, 1870*

The 1870 Ordnance Survey map also reveals that the buildings in the south-west corner of the site served as offices and workshops, with a wall along Rhodeswell Road linking the east end of the workshops to the southern coal store. Both this and the 1862 map show the main entrance to the works on the road to the west, by 1870 renamed Johnson Street. There was a small building immediately north of the entrance, and the Ordnance Survey map shows the isolated building in the north-west corner of the works as L-shaped, and enclosed within a boundary separating it from the works.

In the year after the passage of the 1860 Metropolis Gas Act, the Commercial Company justified a price rise to its customers to 4s 5d per thousand by making arrangements to improve the illuminating power and quality of gas, as required by the new legislation (LMA, B/CGC/5, 55–6 (17 May 1861)). Whitehouse was engaged to erect two iron roofs to 'the new purifying house' for £570 (ibid, 54 (10 May 1861); 55 (17 May 1861)), and a Mr Edie was to erect two scrubbers for £90 (ibid, 54 (10 May 1861)) and the columns and girders for 'the new Purifying Shed' for £80 (ibid, 60 (14 June 1861)). Edie's £795 tender for castings for '4 New Purifiers' was accepted, with Whitehouse supplying the '4 Purifier Covers' at £130 each (ibid, 101 (14 March 1862)). Sam Cutler was paid £350 'on account of Roofs for Purifying Shed' (ibid, 212 (29 April 1864)). By 1865 the works had four square purifiers, each 24ft (7.32m) square and 6ft (1.83m) deep, in which the oxide was placed in three layers each about 18in (0.46m) deep (Colburn 1865, 52). The layers of moistened oxide were placed on wooden gratings or 'sieves', iron being too easily corroded (ibid). Two new purifiers were apparently being erected by 1865, each 18ft by 30ft (5.49 x 9.14m) (ibid). The new buildings are likely to have been B14 and B15, erected on the ground where gasholders IV and V had stood.

The ventilation of the coal stores was improved, with windows installed in the roofs for £100 by Cutler and glazed with 'rough glass' by Lemon (LMA, B/CGC/5, 174 (17 July 1863)). The board also set aside £11,284, with £640 for contingencies, for an 'additional Retort House with Coal Stores', the work to be started immediately (ibid, 213 (13 May 1864)), despite earlier concerns that the requirements of the Metropolitan Board of Works Act would interfere with the construction (ibid, 200 (22 January 1864)).

By 1865 the works had a total of 270 20ft (6.10m) long retorts, set mostly seven to a bench (Colburn 1865, 11; Clegg 1866, 392). The retorts were earthenware, in four pieces cemented with Stourbridge fire clay (Clegg 1866, 141, 392), with three retorts oval in section and four circular. The circular retorts were 15in (0.38m) in diameter, and the oval retorts 21in by 15in (0.53 x 0.38m). The oven consisted of a simple arch of three brickwork rings, with the inner ring of firebricks, carried on 14in (0.36m) piers, 7ft 6in high by 7ft 9in wide and 20ft long (2.29 x 2.36 x 6.10m). The retorts were supported by a series of 9in (0.23m) walls which formed chambers through which the heated air rose via 'nostrils' left in the arch over the fire (Figs 43–45). A flue ran below the two bottom retorts communicating with the chimney shaft. The retorts were heated by a furnace at either end of the oven (ibid, 141) and each

oven of seven retorts could carbonise 2 tons of coal in five hours (ibid, 392). In total, the retorts at the works were capable of consuming a maximum of 1700 tons of coal a week (Colburn 1865, 23) to produce 2.5 million cubic feet (70,792m³) of gas per day (ibid, 52).

Repairs and alterations were also made to the four gasholders occupying the works in the early 1860s. Gasholders then numbered 1 and 2 (probably respectively VII and VIII) were repaired and gasholders 3 and 4 (probably IX and X) provided with new inlet and outlet pipes (LMA, B/CGC/5, 102 (21 March 1862)). Gasholder 2 required further repair to its top, and gasholder 4 required a new top altogether, the latter work tendered for by Whitehouse for £750 (ibid, 107 (25 April 1862)).

A major change to the works in this period was the construction of the largest gasholder at Stepney (XI, below). After its completion the works could boast five gasholders, which were then renumbered, with the new gasholder (XI) becoming 'No. 1', and gasholders IX, X, VII and VIII becoming 2, 3, 4 and 5 respectively. Colburn's 1865 reference to four gasholders omits gasholder XI, presumably because it was either not yet built or in the process of construction when Colburn collected his information. His reference is echoed by Clegg (1866, 392). Colburn refers to the Company having 'four telescopic holders, two being 119ft [36.27m] in diameter each, and 52ft [15.85m] high, while the others are 110ft [33.53m] each by 52ft [15.85m]' (Colburn 1865, 69).

The increase in gas capacity required other changes. A new station meter was to be built by Parkinson for £750, to pass 100,000 cubic feet (2832m³) of gas per hour (LMA, B/CGC/6, 28 (27 January 1865)).

The older gasholders were showing their age. Leaks in gasholders 2 and 3 (IX and X) had to be repaired (LMA, B/CGC/6, 160 (6 December 1867) and the topsheets of the latter also needed attention (ibid, 179 (22 May 1868). A 'new top' to gasholder 4 (VII) was provided by local firm Messrs Cutler and Sons for £775 (LMA, B/CGC/8, 187 (14 March 1873)).

The City of London Gas Act 1868 spurred further changes at the works. This legislation contained clauses relating to the illuminating power and purity of gas manufactured by companies across the metropolis, and the engineer made a report to the board in 1870 about the Commercial's ability to meet these requirements. It had been experimenting with gas purification for a number of years: in 1860, for example, F J Evans licensed the Company to use his patented method for purifying gas (LMA, B/CGC/4, np (25 May 1860)), presumably by iron oxide (Trueman 1997, 15); and other methods for purification had also been tested, for example that adopted by 'Mr Hills, Mr Laming and Mr Warner' (LMA, B/CGC/6, 24 (6 January 1865)). In addition, cannel coal was being extensively used by the Company to enrich the quality of the gas, which was constantly exceeding the statutory minimum of 14½ candles (ibid, 146–7 (23 August 1867)).

The engineer Robert Jones reported that only the 1868 Act's purity clause relating to the presence of sulphur compounds could not be met, because it required a 'Hydrate of Lime'

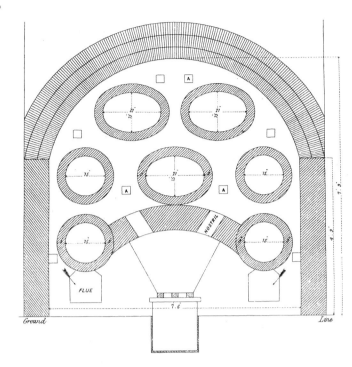

JONES'S SETTING OF SEVEN RETORTS.

Fig 43   Engineer Robert Jones's setting of retorts at Stepney – front elevation (Clegg 1859, 156)

Fig 44   Jones's setting of retorts at Stepney – transverse section (Clegg 1859, 156)

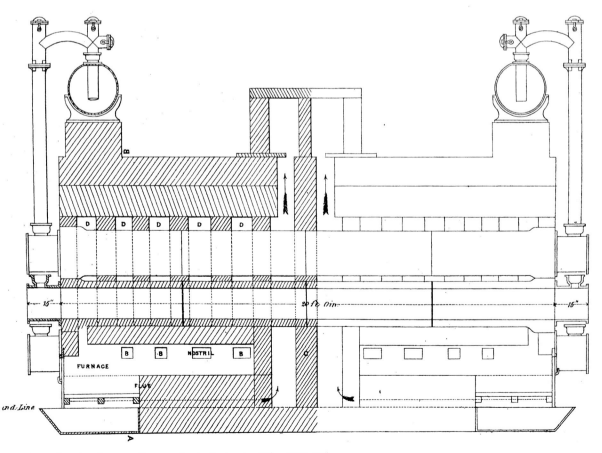

Fig 45   Jones's setting of retorts at Stepney – longitudinal section (Clegg 1859, 156)

process that the Company did not yet possess (LMA, B/CGC/8, 34–6 (25 February 1870)). He had already commissioned a report on the elimination of sulphur from the gas (Colburn 1865, 59–65). A set of lime purifiers of large dimensions was required, Jones said, costing £3000. There would be an economic benefit since the purifiers would also remove carbonic acid, and a smaller amount of cannel coal would be needed to enrich the gas. He also reported that retort houses nos 1 and 2 (probably B8 and B9), in a bad state of repair, required 'reconstruction', adding that the 'new Retort House [B13] would be built on the principle of the last new house [B12] erected five years ago', and adapted so that coal could be delivered by steam power. He recommended that the coal stores should be 'on each side of the Retort House and adapted for the delivery of Coal by steam power'. This would cost £3500. The new coal lift, which would include 'railways, steam lift and travellers', would cost £2500. He proposed to 'remove the Engines and Boilers from the present site to the side of the Canal near to the place where the new purifiers should be erected'. The board approved his plans, which were expected to take 18 months to implement (LMA, B/CGC/8, 34–6 (25 February 1870)).

Lemon was to build the 'New Coal Stores and Retort Houses' (B8, B9, B13), the roofs to be of slate (LMA, B/CGC/8, 41 (8 April 1870)); the volume of the new buildings exceeded 216,000 cubic feet (ibid, 46–7 (3 June 1870)). Lemon received staged payments, of which the final one was made in early 1871 (ibid, 77 (20 January 1871)), so the work was probably completed by then. Aird and Sons' tender of £2000 for the

coal-lifting apparatus was accepted (ibid, 135 (1 March 1872)) and this work seems to have been completed by summer 1872 when a cheque was issued to the company (ibid, 157 (23 August 1872)). The construction of the coal tramway dates to the same year (Ridge 1998, 15). At the time of the MOLA survey, the remains of the tramway consisted of truncated column bases and part of its ground-level base, an open rectangular frame of wrought iron girders. The frame of I-section girders was infilled with concrete (below, 5.7).

Jones made a further report to the board late in 1872. Gas consumption was rising at such a rate that the Company was finding it hard to keep up, even though there were over 60 more retorts in action than during the same period the previous year. He told the board that there was no reserve power in the carbonising department and that drastic action had to be taken. Significantly – although Jones did not state this explicitly – the solution did not lie at the Stepney Works. Instead, he recommended amalgamation with the Ratcliff Company to utilise its reserve power (LMA, B/CGC/8, 166–8 (8 November 1872)). The amalgamation finally took place in 1875. In 1873 the board decided to build a new works and bought land at Poplar for this (ibid, 212 (5 September 1873)). The Company was beginning to shift its focus away from the development of the Stepney Works to elsewhere.

The surveyed structures: gasholder XI

Plans for the new '200ft [60.96m] diameter' gasholder (shown in Fig 46 with subsequent modifications) were approved by the

*Fig 46 View of gasholder 1 (**XI**) looking north-west*

board in 1863 (LMA, B/CGC/5, 160 (1 May 1863)). The construction of this 1.9 million cubic feet (53,802m³) capacity gasholder illustrates the confidence and ambition of the board in these years, since it was for a brief period the third largest in the world, after two of the Imperial Company's gasholders (Tucker 2000, 29).

Thomas Docwra's tender of £11,750 for constructing the tank was successful (LMA, B/CGC/5, 161 (8 May 1863)), with Messrs Oakes providing 'inlet and outlet pipes, connections and guides' for the new gasholder (ibid, 162 (15 May 1863)). Work on the tank was under way by the summer (ibid, 178

(14 August 1863)), with staged payments made during the rest of the year (eg ibid, 179 (21 August 1863); 185 (9 October 1863); 189 (13 November 1863); 196 (1 January 1864)), suggesting that the tank was complete by the beginning of 1864 (Fig 47; Fig 48). The engineer, Robert Jones, was so pleased with the tank, which was particularly watertight, that 'the puddlers' were given a bonus of £10 (LMA, B/CGC/6, 24 (6 January 1865)).

Benjamin Whitehouse was approached directly to build the gasholder itself (LMA, B/CGC/5, 173 (10 July 1863)) and his tender of £13,700 was accepted (ibid, 175 (24 July 1863)). The

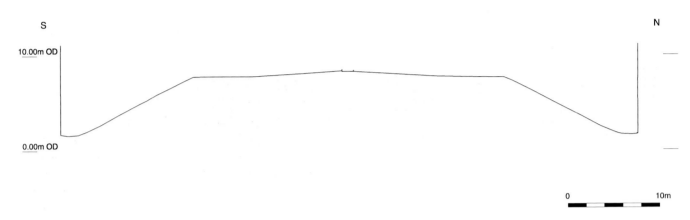

*Fig 47 Cross section through substructure of gasholder 1 (**XI**) (scale 1:400)*

*Fig 48 View looking north-west across the dumpling of gasholder 1 (**XI**)*

top framing of the gasholder was ready for inspection early the following year (ibid, 202 (5 February 1864)), after which his own staged payments (eg ibid, 206 (4 March 1864); 212 (29 April 1864); 217 (10 June 1864)) suggest that the gasholder was completed by summer 1864.

The MOLA survey found that gasholder **XI** was built of 22 guide-frame columns, 9.18m (30ft 1in) apart. Like twin gasholders **IX** and **X**, gasholder **XI** was originally of the giant single-order, single-tier type, Type 11 in Tucker's classification (Tucker 2000, 29), with free-standing columns linked only at their tops with wrought iron girders. The tapering columns were styled in the Tuscan order, with large torus-type bases for stability set on cast iron plinths (Fig 49). The circular below-ground tank was 63.16m (207ft 3in) diameter internally and 9.47m (31ft 1in) deep. It was lined with regularly coursed bricks in English Cross bond. The top of the dumpling was 6.68m (21ft 11in) above the base of the tank.

*Fig 49 Oblique view of the column base of gasholder 1 (**XI**) looking north*

5.6 The late 19th century, 1875–99

Documentary and cartographic evidence

In the last quarter of the 19th century the focus of the Commercial's development increasingly shifted from Stepney to the Poplar Works, although the Stepney Works was still carbonising 2000 tons of coal a week (Glenny Crory 1876, 33). Harry Jones (1843–1926) had been in charge of the Ratcliff Works, becoming the Commercial's deputy engineer after amalgamation in 1875 and working alongside his father Robert, whom he succeeded as engineer five years later (Tucker 2000, 92). Harry had clear ideas about gasworks, and particularly gasholder design, which he expressed in a paper to the Institution of Civil Engineers in 1875 (Jones 1875, quoted in Tucker 2000, 96). In his paper he strongly criticised the 'heavy cylindrical columns with inadequate bases' that were still regularly used. Indeed the 1864 gasholder 1 (**XI**) at Stepney, designed by his father, was of that type – the conservative, giant single-order, single-tier variety (Tucker 2000, 96). There was more room at Poplar for Harry to put his ideas into practice and the major innovations of this period of the Company's history took place there. If it was at Stepney that Robert Jones made his mark with the reconstruction of the works in the 1850s and 1870s, then Poplar was the place where his son could do the same. Nonetheless, important alterations were made to three of the Stepney gasholders in the 1870s.

The engineer reported to the board that as a consequence of the Company's 1875 Act, the system of purification would need to be altered. The board instructed him 'to convert the old Coal Store into a purifying shed and to increase the present purifiers' (LMA, B/CGC/10, 102 (3 September 1875)). Work on the purifiers was undertaken by Messrs Bennet, who were paid £338 in summer 1877 (LMA, B/CGC/12, np (15 June 1877)). The retort settings were periodically renewed, with clay retorts and firebrick purchased (eg LMA, B/CGC/14, 26 (15 December 1882)), the orders usually being split between three or so companies (eg LMA, B/CGC/15, 226 (23 December 1887)). One significant development was the installation of two sets of carburetted water gas (CWG) plant from 1897, each set capable of generating 1 million cubic feet (28,317m³) of gas a day (Stewart 1957, 98).

Repair of the offices was undertaken for £420 by Lemon (LMA, B/CGC/12, 24 (29 June 1877)), who had built coal stores and retort houses at the works six years earlier. His tender of £750 for extending the head office at Stepney to provide a showroom for stoves and providing additional office accommodation was accepted (LMA, B/CGC/14, 10 (27 October 1882)). Eight years later, a plan 'for the Alteration of the Company's offices' at Stepney for £500 was approved (LMA, B/CGC/16, 115 (12 December 1890)). Various pieces of plant were purchased during this period, but the minutes do not always specify the works for which they were intended. For example, a gas-powered crane was procured from Messrs Hunter and English for £400 (LMA, B/CGC/14, np (23 May

1884)), but it is unclear whether this was for Stepney. The board did approve a 15 horsepower steam engine for the exhauster at Stepney, however, at a cost of no more than £200 (LMA, B/CGC/15, 156 (3 June 1887)). The gantry along the canal front was strengthened for £440, 'Two Cranes and Three Grabs' were purchased for £980, and a 'Stoves Repairing Shop and Store' (B17) were erected for £950 (LMA, B/CGC/16, 481 (13 December 1894)).

The Goad insurance map of 1891 (Fig 50) provides useful interior detail for the buildings at the works and illustrates how the works had developed from the previous period, particularly when compared with the Ordnance Survey map of some 20 years earlier (above, Fig 42). The arrangement for delivering coal to the coal stores had been upgraded, and was now by coal tramway elevated 24ft (7.3m) high on cast iron columns. Two hydraulic cranes transferred coal into the coal stores of retort houses nos 2, 3 and 4 (respectively B13, B9 and B8). The tramway also extended around the northernmost coal stores of retort house no. 1 (B12). The design of retort houses 1 and 2 (B12 and B13) was similar, with the top-lit coal stores flanking the retort house, which was equipped with a central chimney. Retort house 3 and 4, each with a chimney at its east gable end, had a long central area for coal storage, although most of the coal would have come from the large coal store to the south. This coal store had been extended westwards since 1870 and included a stokers' lobby.

By 1891 the coal store that fronted directly on to the canal in 1870 had been converted to house new purifiers, and a 20

horsepower engine and exhauster house (B16), with the engine moved from its former more central position in what was now the coal store of retort house no. 2 (B13). In addition to the new purifiers, new scrubbers and washers had been built and the purifying house east of gasholder 2 (IX) extended westwards. Other purifiers had been demolished to be replaced by one of two areas for storing coke.

The Goad plan adopts the same numbering scheme for the gasholders – labelled 'Gasometers' – as the Company. Gasholder 1 (XI) is indicated as being 80ft (24.4m) high, with a capacity of 2,528,000 cubic feet (71,600m³). The height seems to be an error, since the MOLA survey found this gasholder to be 90ft (27.4m) high, and no heightening of gasholder 1 is known after the date of the map. Gasholders 2 and 3 (IX and X) are both indicated as 52ft (15.8m) high with a capacity of 572,000 cubic feet (16,200m³) and gasholders 4 and 5 (VII and VIII) as 52ft (15.8m) high, each with a capacity of 400,000 cubic feet (11,300m³).

Other buildings had been constructed or changed their use since 1870. Although the offices at the south-west corner of the works were retained (B10), the workshop (B6) running along Ben Jonson Road (formerly Rhodeswell Road) had been converted into a top-lit meter house with rooms for engineers on the first floor and carpenters on the second. By 1891 the building (B18) to the north of the offices was a store, more buildings had been constructed along the west boundary of the works and there was a smithy in the north-east corner (B19).

The surveyed structures: alterations to gasholders IX–XI

Although no more gasholders were built at the works in the final quarter of the 19th century, storage was still an issue. As the cramped works could not extend laterally, the only choice was to extend upwards. As a result, in early 1886 the board accepted Clayton Sons and Co's tender of £6163 to heighten gasholder 1 (XI) from two lifts to three (LMA, B/CGC/14, 418 (5 February 1886)). Staged payments were made until late that year (LMA, B/CGC/15, 58 (3 September 1886)) when presumably the work was complete. The capacity of the gasholder leapt by almost one-third to 2,528,000 cubic feet (71,600m³).

Horizontal girders and diagonal tie rods were added to the gasholder, converting it into a Type 18A (Tucker 2000, 10, 13) (Fig 51). The MOLA survey found that the columns tapered as they progressed upwards from each tier of girders: below the lower tier of girders they had a diameter of 0.91m (36in); below the middle tier of girders a diameter of 0.84m (33in); and below the upper tier of girders a diameter of 0.69m (27in). At their widest, the column bases were 1.61m (5ft 3in) in diameter. The columns did not correspond stylistically to their bases, but simply had shafts which enter the plain cylindrical capitals. Neck rings were present below the tops of the capitals and the columns were articulated from five separate sections.

The girders conformed to Type H, as defined by Tucker, a style of girder dating from c 1860–90 (Tucker 2000, 12).

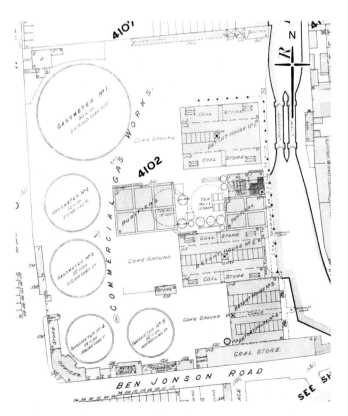

Fig 50 The Goad insurance map, 1891, showing the Commercial Gasworks (LMA/SC/GL/GOA/VOL/XII/1891, 378)

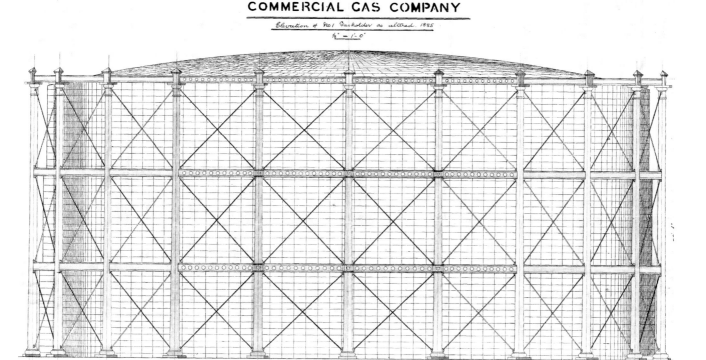

COMMERCIAL GAS COMPANY

Elevation of No1 Gasholder as altered. 1885

½" = 1'-0"

*Fig 51 Elevation of gasholder 1 (**XI**) 'as altered 1885' (NGA, NT, COG/E/T/7)*

The lower two tiers of girders were bolted to collars that clasped the columns, so the heads of the bolts were flush with the alignment of the girder. The collars bore the badge of the Commercial Company (Fig 52). The top tier of girders was fixed to the column capitals with bolts at right angles to the girder, and secured to base plates on the cap. The horizontal girders were of I-section, and composed of perforated plates which were riveted to the sections that formed the flanges. The girders of the lower tier were 8.05m (26ft 5in) long, 0.81m (32in) high and 0.28m (11in) deep; those of the middle tier were 8.18m (26ft 10in) long, 0.76m (30in) high and 0.28m (11in) deep; and those of the top tier 8.46m (27ft 9in) long, 0.76m (30in) high and 0.28m (11in) deep. Each girder had 12 circular perforations; the lower tier girders comprised two riveted-together sectional plates, whereas each top tier girder had four plates.

The perforations in the top tier were larger (15in or 0.38m) than those of the other tiers (12in or 0.30m), no doubt to reduce the weight of the girder. The lower tier at centre was 9.26m (30ft 5in) from the second tier at centre, while the second was 9.32m (30ft 7in) from the top tier at centre. Further structural stability was provided above each tier and between each column in the form of diagonal rods.

The bell of this gasholder could not be recorded in detail as it had been previously removed during demolition, as had the timber rest frame (Fig 53). In this case the bell was telescopic,

with three lifts present. The inner lift had a diameter of 60.66m (199ft), the middle 61.67m (202ft 4in) and the outer 62.53m (205ft 2in). Mounted on to the internal face of the tank were vertical, regularly spaced cast iron guide posts (Fig 54). These were set 5.41m (17ft 9in) apart at centre. They were bolted on to stone blocks that extended into the brickwork.

Three types of guide post were present (Fig 55), referred to here as Types 1–3. The Type 1 and 2 guide posts were 7.81m (25ft 7in) long overall and were formed of two sections, the top being 4.57m (15ft) long and the lower 3.75m (12ft 4in) long. The width of the internal channel was 150mm (6in). The Type 3 guide posts were of Type 1 profile, but modified by the addition of a fitting narrowing the channel width. The Type 2 guide posts were associated with replacement guide columns that were not original to the structure. Underneath each guide post, inside the inner edge of the tank at its base, was a series of flat metal plates which acted as the base plates for the lift mechanism. When the bell was contracted, the lifts would rest on these plates. Although obscured by water within the tank, these were recorded (Fig 6 shows the general arrangement).

The board also subsequently accepted a tender from W D Howard for 'the renewal and extension' of two of the gasholders for £13,960 (LMA, B/CGC/16, 261 (22 July 1892)): gasholder 2 (**IX**) and its twin gasholder 3 (**X**) were heightened from two lifts to three (Fig 56; Fig 57). The specifications for this work are dated respectively February and April 1892 (NGA, NT,

*Fig 52 Orthogonal view showing typical detail of a collar on the middle tier of girders of gasholder 1 (**XI**)*

*Fig 53 The timber rest frame structure of gasholder 1 (**XI**) during demolition (Glendee 2004)*

*Fig 54 The tank substructure of gasholder 1 (**XI**) looking north, showing the arrangement of guide posts*

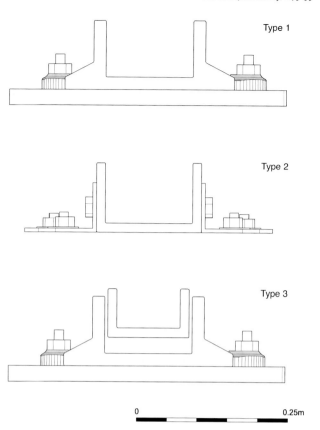

Type 1

Type 2

Type 3

0   0.25m

*Fig 55 Profiles of guide posts in the tank substructure of gasholder 1 (**XI**) (scale 1:6)*

COG/E/P/1; COG/E/P/2) and contain useful information about how the work was to be achieved. The guide framing in both gasholders was to be heightened 'by the insertion of 2 pieces of column 11ft 8in [3.56m] long each and of similar pattern to the existing Column between the present top length of the Column and the length it at present rests upon'. This confirms the hypothesis that the existing columns were heightened in this way (Tucker 2000, 52). The two inserted columns (Fig 58) increased the height of each existing column by 23ft 4in (7.11m). Additional horizontal girders 'formed of ½ inch [12.7mm] web plate' were also added, and the top tier of cast iron girders and their caps were replaced with girders of wrought iron. The new girders were to be 'clasped on the columns by ornamental castings'. The new sections of columns and new girders were not

the only additions. Both gasholders were provided with 'three tiers of 44 Diagonal Tie Rods' in steel. Originally of the giant single-order, single-tier guide frame, Type 11, the gasholders were converted to Type 18A (ibid, 29).

This corresponds with the results of the MOLA survey. This found that both gasholders were 23.37m (76ft 8in) high, measured from the underside of the base to the top of the column. The columns of both gasholders consisted of five sections, linked by three tiers of horizontal girders and stabilised by diagonal tie rods. Like those of gasholder **XI**, the columns tapered with height: the column diameter was 0.91m (36in) below the lower tier of horizontal girders, 0.84m (33in) below the middle tier of girders and 0.76m (30in) below the upper tier. In contrast to the bases, the capitals were plain cylindrical caps.

The perforated horizontal girders linking the columns were I-shaped in section, their short edges riveted to plates to form flanges. The girders of the lower tier were 7.54m (24ft 9in) long, 0.69m (27in) high and 0.25m (10in) deep; in the middle tier they were 7.54m (24ft 9in) long, 0.69m (27in) high and 0.25m (10in) deep; and in the upper tier they were 7.92m (26ft) long, 0.69m (27in) high and 0.25m (10in) deep. The lower tier was 7.64m (25ft 1in) below the second tier, which was 7.59m (24ft 11in) below the top tier. The girders conform to Tucker's Type H, dating to c 1860–90 (Tucker 2000, 12, 16).

In the lower two tiers the girders were attached to the columns with bolts fixed to collars clasping the columns, so the heads of the bolts were flush with the web of the girder. The

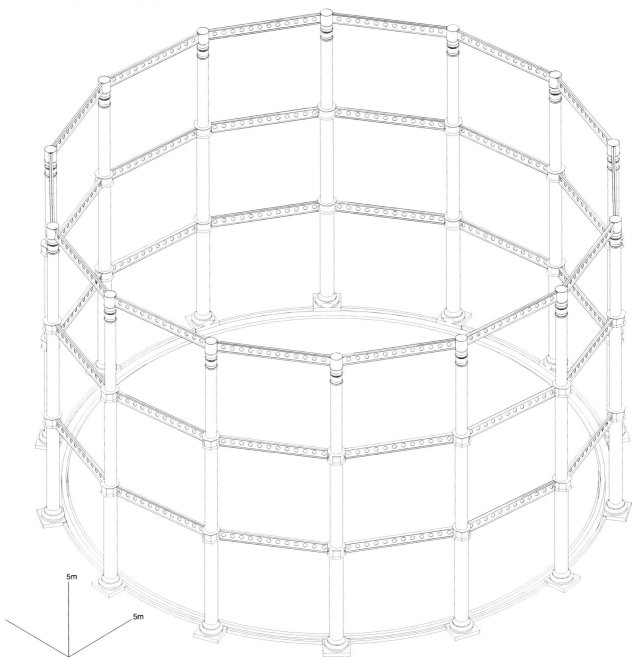

*Fig 56 Isometric view of gasholder 3 (**X**) (scale 1:250)*

top tier was bolted to the cylindrical cap at right angles to the girder, through L-sections set between two ends of the girders and vertical plates on the cap. The distinctive, ornamented cast iron collars bore the badge of the Commercial Company, but in a different style from that recorded on later gasholder 1 (**XI**) (Fig 59).

The specifications for the renewal and extension of gasholders 2 (**IX**) and 3 (**X**) (NGA, NT, COG/E/P/1) differ significantly only in the description of the work on their respective bells. The bell to gasholder 2 was to be scrapped and an entirely new one built; in gasholder 3, only the top lift was to be removed, and the lower lift retained. In gasholder 2, the upper lift was to be 119ft 3in (36.35m) diameter by 26ft (7.92m) high, the middle lift 121ft 3in (36.96m) diameter by 25ft 8in (7.82m) high and the bottom lift 123ft 3in (37.57m) diameter and 25ft 4in (7.72m)

high. In gasholder 3, the upper lift was to be 118ft 8in (36.17m) diameter by 26ft (7.92m) high, the middle lift 120ft 11in (36.86m) diameter by 26ft (7.92m) high and the bottom lift 122ft 4in (37.29m) by 25ft 4in (7.72m) high. The crowns of both bells were to be 'formed to a true segment of a sphere rising from the chord of the curb 9 feet [2.74m] to the centre'.

Aesthetics were not forgotten in the specifications. The bells of both gasholders were to have two coats of red oxide of iron paint, and the girders and columns two coats of antimony stone colour paint.

In addition to these major alterations, from time to time gasholder 2 (**IX**) needed repair. Repairs were undertaken by Messrs Piggott for £500 in 1877 (LMA, B/CGC/12, 52 (17 August 1877)) and further repairs were needed in the final decade of the century (LMA, B/CGC/16 (238 (25 March 1892)).

*Fig 57 Orthogonal view
looking north-west of a typical
collar on the middle tier of
girders of gasholder 3 (**X**)*

*Fig 58 Detail of inserted column in guide frames to gasholders 2 (**IX**) and 3 (**X**) (NGA, NT, COG/E/T/2)*

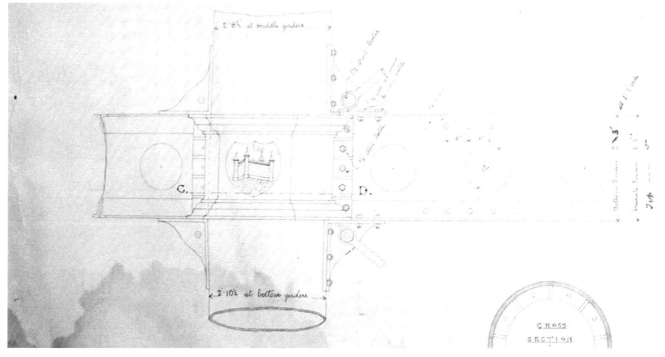

*Fig 59 Detail of new collars and girders to gasholders 2 (**IX**) and 3 (**X**) (NGA, NT, COG/E/T/2)*

5.7 The early 20th century, 1900–49

In the 20th century, parts of the works were modernised or rebuilt. At the turn of the century 'the erection of an additional Oil Gas Plant' at the works was approved (LMA, B/CGC/17, 328 (25 January 1900)). The CWG plant at Stepney was completed in October 1900 at a cost of £16,136 (*J Gas Sup*, 9 April 1901). Such plants had also been erected at the Company's Poplar and Wapping stations by 1898 (LMA, B/CGC/17, 140 (11 February 1897); 213 (24 March 1898)). The advantage of CWG plant was that a large amount of gas could be made with relatively small apparatus. This gave a gas manager the flexibility to deal with unexpected peaks in demand, for example during fog, as well as dispensing with the necessity to store large volumes of gas in gasholders at a works.

The handling of raw materials had been increasingly mechanised by the first decade of the 20th century. Coal was lifted from barges by stationary or travelling cranes and grabs on a gantry (*J Gas Sup*, 28 April 1908, 278). This arrangement had replaced the 1870s cast iron coal tramway (Fig 60) in 1897 and was used until 1912 (Ridge 1998, 2). The coal was dropped into a hopper to be crushed by a gas-driven breaker and then fed into trucks on a weighbridge. The trucks were lifted by one of two gas-powered lifts, to run along elevated rails and shoot the coal into the 800 ton capacity overhead coal store of the principal retort house (no. 2, B13) (*J Gas Sup*, 28 April 1908, 278) (Fig 61 and below, Fig 67).

Retort house no. 2 was also mechanised. In 1904 it was agreed to convert it from having eight sets of hand-charged retorts to 16 sets of machine-charged retorts, at an estimated cost of £11,200 (LMA, B/CGC/18, 18 (3 March 1904)). By 1908 there were two benches with 16 settings of ten retorts, each D-section retort measuring 22in by 15in by 20ft long (0.56 x 0.38 x 6.10m) (*J Gas Sup*, 28 April 1908, 277). The De Brouwer charging machine, installed in 1904 (LMA, B/CGC/18, 36 (7 July 1904)), was suspended in a framework and ran on rails, with a hopper in the top to receive coal from the overhead coal

Fig 61 The coal conveyor in the early 20th century (Co-partnership H, December 1932, 224)

Fig 60 View of what may be the truncated iron base of the 1870s coal tramway, looking south

stores. The coke was pushed out by one of two Ludbrook pushers, falling into the basement of the retort house to be sorted on a travelling screen and then carted out through archways in the side of the house. These pushers were patented by – and named after – the Engineer Stanley H Jones's assistant at the works (*J Gas Sup*, 28 April 1908, 278).

Retort house no. 2 had the capacity to produce over 2.5 million cubic feet (71,000m³) of gas a day. The three other retort houses (B12, B9 and B8), still only equipped with hand-worked settings in 1908 but each capable of producing 0.75 million cubic feet (21,238m³) a day, were kept in reserve. When the two CWG plants of the Humphreys and Glasgow type, each with a capacity of 1 million cubic feet (28,317m³) a day, were taken into account, the works as a whole could produce 6.75 million cubic feet (191,139m³) of gas a day (*J Gas Sup*, 28 April 1908, 277–8).

Retorts in retort house no. 2 (B13) were reconstructed again in 1912 (LMA, B/CGC/18, 392 (8 January 1912)), when the Company started using steam wagons to bring coal by road from its Wapping Works (Ridge 1998, 2). Two years later the retorts were converted to regenerative furnaces (LMA, B/CGC/19, 23 (2 April 1914)). Much later retort house no. 3 (B9) was mechanised when a Drake charging machine and a De Brouwer charging machine were installed (LMA, B/CGC/22, 108 (5 October 1933); 115 (2 November 1933)) (Fig 62).

In 1903 an office extension (B10) costing £650 was approved (LMA, B/CGC/17, 490 (25 June 1903) and later the rental offices

were extended to absorb the governor and meter room (B6), which was shifted to the oil gas meter house (B20) at a cost of £2000 (LMA, B/CGC/18, 335 (9 March 1911)). A second-hand boiler and coal breaker, costing a total of £1500, were installed at the works in 1918 (LMA, B/CGC/19, 360 (28 March 1919)).

There were further alterations in the 1930s (*Co-partnership H*, April 1935, 173) (Fig 63), including workshops for the gas sales department (B21) and renewal of the purification plant. The foundations of the 'four existing' tower scrubbers were found to be unsafe and the tower scrubbers were replaced by 'washer scrubbers of the rotary type' (LMA, B/CGC/22, 241 (4 April 1935)). One of these rotary scrubbers was to be used to extract ammonia and another to extract naphthalene. The Whessoe Foundry and Engineering Company won the tender to erect the scrubbers for £3700 (ibid, 245 (18 April 1935)). In 1936 it was decided to replace the coal lift at the canal end of retort house no. 2 with an elevator supplied and erected by the Moxey Conveyor Company (LMA, B/CGC/22, 386 (10 December 1936)).

The annual output of the works in 1913 was 720 million cubic feet (20,388,130m³), and in 1939 this had risen to 1000 million cubic feet (28,316,847m³) (Stewart 1957, 98). However, the Company claimed in 1935 that all three of the Commercial's works were capable of generating over 8000 million cubic feet (226,534,773m³) a year in total (*Co-partnership H*, September 1935, 149), more than eight times Stepney's output a few years later. This suggests that by the 1930s the Stepney Works was a minor, albeit significant, contributor to the total amount of gas

Fig 62 A charging machine in operation inside a retort house at the works in the 1930s (Co-partnership H, *April 1932, 25*)

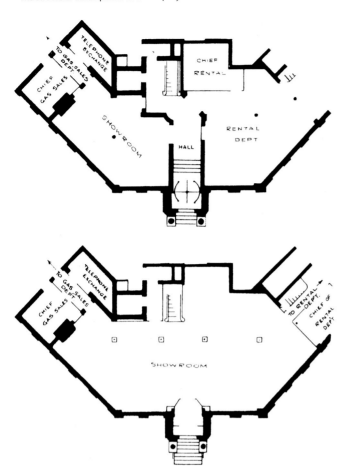

Fig 63 *Plans of the head office before (top) and after alterations in 1931*
(Co-partnership H, *April 1931, 49–50*)

Fig 64 *Mains laying in the 1930s (*Co-partnership H, *October 1932, 170)*

produced by the Company.

Like other parts of the works, the gasholders were showing their considerable age by the 1920s. The top lift of gasholder 5 (**VIII**) required repairs estimated at £4000–£5000 (LMA, B/CGC/20, 62 (8 April 1920)), and metal deterioration in the roof framing and 'the slipping of the clay mound in the centre of the tank' also caused problems (ibid, 133 (15 January 1921)). Gas mains also required periodic replacement (Fig 64).

More seriously, in 1923 the bell of gasholder 4 (**VII**), built by Horton in 1851 and at the time being used as an oil gas relief holder, collapsed after too much gas was drawn off (LMA, B/CGC/20, 329 (14 June 1923)). The trussing buckled, the sheets tore and the irreparably damaged holder had to be demolished. The tender to build a new gasholder (**XII**) with an additional lift was won by London-based Cutler and Sons (ibid, 464 (5 March 1925)). Cutler also built gasholder 3 at the Company's Poplar Works in 1928–9 (Tucker 2000, 93), and the two gasholders share features, although the Stepney example has an underground tank. The engineer insisted that only wrought iron be used – remarkable at this date – rejecting any use of steel or rust-resistant Armco iron (LMA, B/CGC/20, 472 (2 April 1925)) even though this increased the price by almost £1000 to £18,040 (ibid, 472 (16 April 1925)).

The specification for the work (NGA, NT, COG/E/P/1, March 1925), signed by Samuel Cutler and the Commercial's

chairman William Bradshaw, stipulated that the contractor 'take down and remove the whole of the existing C.I. [cast iron] columns and cross girders', taking care that 'the existing holding down bolts are not damaged in any way so that they may be utilised for the new Holder'. The contractor was 'to supply and fix 24 Tank Guides' in the existing tank, which was to be reused once it was cleaned out. The diameters of the five lifts were to be 91ft 8in (27.94m) for the upper lift; 94ft 3in (28.73m) for the second lift; 94ft 10in (28.91m) for the third lift; 99ft 5in (30.30m) for the fourth lift; and 102ft (31.09m) for the lower lift. All were to be 25ft 9in (7.85m) high, apart from the lower lift which was to be 25ft 7in (7.80m) high. The crown of the holder was to be 'a true segment of a sphere rising from the chord of a curb 5ft [1.52m] to the centre, ie of a radius of 212' 3" [64.69m]'.

The guide framing was to consist of 12 main standards connected by five tiers of cross girders and braced by two diagonal ties in each panel. The standards were to have an overall height of 130ft 1in (39.65m), measured from the underside of the base plate to the top of the finial, and to taper from 4ft (1.22m) wide at the base plate to 2ft (0.61m) at 128ft (39.01m). Like other gasholders at the works, 'red oxide paint [was] to be used on bell and stone colour on framing'. The new gasholder 4 (**XII**) was completed after February 1926 (LMA, B/CGC/21, 39 (18 February 1926)) and gasholder 5 (**VIII**) became the new oil gas relief holder.

The new gasholder 4 (Fig 65; Fig 66) was not surveyed in detail by MOLA as it did not date from the Victorian era use of the site. The five lifts, the outermost of which was fixed to the inside face of the tank, were found to measure (from the outer lift in) 31.09m, 30.33m, 29.57m, 28.80m and 28.04m in diameter.

Cutler and Sons also won a tender to repair the large gasholder 1 (**XI**) for £12,961 (LMA, B/CGC/21, 401 (12 March 1931)). The whole crown had to be renewed, the grip of the outer lift and all cups and rollers had to be replaced, the guide channels on the framing had to be refixed and additional stiffeners had to be fitted to all three lifts (NGA, NT, COG/E/P/1, May 1931). The work was finished by late 1933 (LMA, B/CGC/22, 108 (5 October 1933)).

New internal stiffeners and guide rollers were required for gasholder 2 (**IX**) in the mid 1930s; the work was done by Messrs Westwood and Wright for £3550 (LMA, B/CGC/22, 268 (11 July 1935)). The specification detailed how carriages on the inner, middle and outer lifts were to be altered, reused or replaced, how modifications were also to be made to the bottom curb carriages, and how existing stiffeners were to be supplemented by new ones (NGA, NT, COG/E/P/1, 26 June 1935).

The Company estimated that the Second World War cost it £937,000 (LMA, B/CGC/23, 439 (5 February 1948)). Gasholder 2 (**IX**) was extensively damaged by enemy action and had to be repaired by Cutler and Sons. The outer lift was scrapped (ibid,

*Fig 65   View of gasholder 4 (**XII**) from the north-east*

*Fig 66   View looking south-west across the dumpling of gasholder 4 (**XII**)*

118 (13 March 1941)) and gasholder 3 (**X**) was also reduced to two lifts. Damage to gasholder 1 (**XI**) was even worse, and (unspecified) parts of it were requisitioned by the Ministry of Works (ibid, 219 (23 September 1943)). After the war, Cutler and Sons' tender of £16,175 to reconstruct this gasholder was accepted (ibid, 354 (25 July 1946)). A high explosive bomb also dropped between gasholders 3 and 4, resulting in the replacement of one of the columns in the south-east quadrant of gasholder 3's guide frame (Ridge 1998, 12). A fire in the

water gas engine room caused £1500 worth of damage (LMA, B/CGC/23, 292 (26 July 1945)).

Gas making at Stepney ceased on 9 September 1945, and the Company's district was supplied with 'no difficulty' from the Poplar Works from that date (LMA, B/CGC/23, 305 (18 October 1945)). The works closed completely the following year, although it remained a gasholder station, for the storage of gas produced elsewhere (Stewart 1957, 98) (Fig 67). It was the Poplar Works that now had priority, and plant transferred to

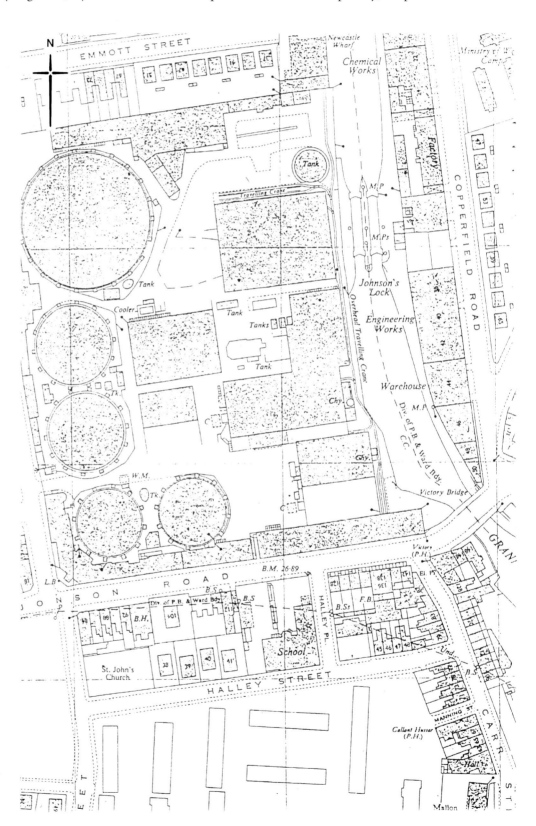

Fig 67 Detail from the 1947 Ordnance Survey map showing the Stepney Works, since 1945 used as a gasholder station

that works from Stepney included a De Brouwer retort charging machine and pushers, electric generating sets, a 1–20 ton weighbridge, machine tools, two Broomwade steam driven air compressors, 13 electric and steam pumps, a steel water tank, two portable coal elevators, a Neckar water softening plant, two horizontal steam engines, three exhausters and a platers' shop (LMA, B/CGC/23, 389 (3 April 1947)). 1949 saw the nationalisation of the gas manufacturing industry, and the Commercial Company became part of the North Thames Gas Board.

5.8   After 1949

Gasholders 1 to 4 (**IX–XII**) remained in use for gas storage. According to Ordnance Survey mapping, gasholder 5 (**VIII**) was demolished between 1951 and 1954, while the other

structures on the site, including all coal stores and retort houses, were demolished between 1947 and 1952, leaving only a few building frontages along Harford Street and Ben Jonson Road as part of the site perimeter. The Stepney gasholder station closed in the early 1990s.

During the decontamination and redevelopment of the site from June 2002 to March 2005, most surviving parts of the Stepney Works, including the last four gasholders, were swept away. Some elements of the gasworks remain, including parts of the boundary wall along Ben Jonson Road and the canalside tramway base. Some of the new streets and residential blocks bear names that reflect former times – Candle Street, Coalstore Court, Horseley Court and Tramway Court – but all that survives of the gasholders that once dominated the local London skyline are four re-erected column bases and cut-down columns from the guide frame of gasholder 2 (**IX**) (Fig 68) and, mounted on the new buildings, several of the Company's decorative shields (cf Fig 52) from the first tier of girders of its guide frame.

Fig 68 The site of the gasworks after redevelopment, with re-erected column bases of gasholder 2 (IX) (photo Michael Bussell)

6

The impact of the Commercial Company

6.1 Impact on the public domain

The provision of street lighting was the earliest and most obvious effect of the gas industry on the public domain, with local parishes allowing gas companies to lay mains in exchange for providing cheap public lighting. Gas street light was praised as being 'little inferior to daylight', in contrast to the 'dismal' light from oil lamps (Stewart 1958, 43). The gas companies were not averse to boosting this business by playing on parochial bodies' fear of crime. When John Hammack, the chairman of the Ratcliff Company, was trying to pressurise the Commissioners of St George's Pavement to reconsider their decision to allow the Commercial to enter their district, he claimed that gaslight was 'a necessary appendage to the police'. He claimed: 'It is an admitted fact that Gas Lights not only afford Great Protection to the inhabitants, but are preventatives to the Commission of Crime, a street now lighted with Oil would afford great inducements for the perpetration of outrage and robbery' (LBTH, L/SGE/J/4/30, letter of 22 October 1840).

The technology of street lighting improved over time. A major innovation was the upright mantle, and high efficiency burners using the regenerative principle were developed by Welsbach and Lucas in 1900, in 1905 by Selas and in 1907 by Keith and Blackman (Stewart 1958, 46). The latter could be used to supply lanterns of 3000–4500 candle power (ibid, 46–7).

The lives of local people were bound up with that of the Commercial Company. The Stepney Works is even memorialised in the windows of nearby St Dunstan's Church, where the gasholders are depicted in the east window among the streets bombed in the Second World War (Ridge 1998, 12). The Commercial was a major employer, and frequently there were two or three generations working for the Company (ibid, 5), their wages feeding back into the local economy. In 1846 a stoker was paid 26s a week (LMA, B/CGC/1, 428 (29 July 1846)), rising to 29s in 1853, when a firemen was paid 30s a week (LMA, B/CGC/3, 270 (12 August 1853)). In 1859 the weekly wage of a stoker was 30s, a coke-hole man 24s 6d and a coke wheeler 21s (Maddocks 1931, 221). In 1850, a foreman was appointed at £120 a year (LMA, B/CGC/2, 298 (25 November 1850)), his £2 6s weekly pay contrasting with that of a messenger at 7s 6d a week (ibid, 309 (23 January 1851)). At the top of the scale, the Company's engineer Robert Jones was paid £1500 a year in 1873 (LMA, B/CGC/8, 194 (9 May 1873)), a six-figure sum in today's (2010) terms, and somewhat more than his son Harry, who inherited his position seven years later and was paid £1405 a year (LMA, B/CGC/14, 32–3 (5 January 1883)). Even so, this was over four times the amount paid to the manager of the Poplar Works, Mr Ludbrook, whose salary was £310 a year at the time. A lower end professional, Mr Bickley, a rental clerk, was paid £70 a year (ibid).

A proposal by a board member to establish a 'fund for the relief in sickness and accident' of workers in the Company's employ (LMA, B/CGC/2, 97 (12 May 1848)) was withdrawn because of difficulties 'in consequence of the few workmen regularly employed on the Works' (ibid, 121 (18 August 1848)).

Even so, the Company periodically paid out for accidents, for example £5 to the widow of a worker killed in the engine house (LMA, B/CGC/3, 395 (12 May 1854)). A 'Benefit Society for the Company's Workmen' was set up in 1859, with the Company donating £100 a year (Maddocks 1931, 223; LMA, B/CGC/4, 185–6 (14 October 1859)). The Company paid £60 into the 'Workmen's Fund' in 1883 (LMA, B/CGC/14, 102 (20 July 1883)) and made regular payments of this order over the next few years to the 'Workmen's Club' (eg LMA, B/CGC/14, 202 (30 May 1884); 307 (10 April 1885); B/CGC/15, 229 (30 December 1887)).

In 1885 the board awarded ten 'decayed and infirm workmen' weekly superannuation allowances averaging 6s 10d. The average age of these labourers, lamplighters, a stoker, a fireman, a cannel breaker and an engine driver was 68 years. Between them the ten had 287 years' service; the oldest, aged 80, had worked for the Company half his life (LMA, B/CGC/14, 308 (10 April 1885)). In 1901 the Company started a profit-sharing scheme; this developed into a co-partnership scheme in 1927 (Ridge 1998, 5) which aimed for 'the thorough union of capital and labour' (*Co-partnership H*, August 1931, 137). A pension fund was introduced in 1919 (LMA, B/CGC/19, 499 (28 August 1919)).

As well as providing jobs for hundreds of men, many of the proprietors (shareholders) would have come from the area surrounding the works and would have been consumers of the Company's gas (Maddocks 1931, 64–5). In the early 1840s there were some 500 proprietors, of whom at least 200 each held fewer than ten £5 shares. In the first decade of the Company's operation, a great many consumers were local tradespeople, for example public houses (LMA, B/CGC/2, 103 (2 June 1848); 110

(30 June 1848)), and other consumers included hospitals and asylums (ibid, 147 (22 December 1848)), police stations, breweries, schools, places of worship, workhouses and sweatshops (Maddocks 1931, 89).

Like many Victorian undertakings, the Commercial made regular charitable donations. Early examples included £5 5s to Mile End School, £2 2s to Bishopsgate School (LMA, B/CGC/1, 55, 57 (28 August 1844)), and – perhaps not surprisingly given that the Company's nickname was 'The Licensed Victuallers' Company' (Chapter 4.2) – £10 10s to the Licensed Victuallers' Asylum (ibid, 163 (23 April 1845)). Donations to a variety of causes continued down the years, for example £5 to the 'King Ragged School' in 1872 (LMA, B/CGC/8, 147 (28 June 1872)). However, the Company was not deterred from taking action against defaulters, however worthy the cause. In 1870 it cut off Mile End Old Town Ragged School's gas until the bill was paid, although it did agree to waive half the outstanding amount (ibid, 39 (18 March 1870)).

Later in its history, the Company established a sports and social club with a gymnasium from 1932, called the Co-partnership Institute, 1.75 km south-east of the Stepney Works at the corner of East India Dock Road and Hale Street. In 1934–6 the Company built Malam Gardens next door, to provide accommodation for some of its workers. The development of 29 two-storey cottages in three rows along three private lanes, originally completely gas-powered, still survives (Cherry et al 2005, 650; Ridge 1998, 5) (Fig 69).

Some impacts on the public domain were wholly unintended, although fortunately there were no explosions as serious as the one at the London Gas Light Company's Nine Elms Works in 1865 that destroyed the meter house and a gasholder, killing at

*Fig 69 The Commercial Company's housing estate at Malam Gardens, built 1934–6 (*Co-partnership H*, May 1936, 67)*

least ten workers and wrecking local houses (*Illustrated London News*, 4, 11, 18 November 1865, quoted in Everard 1949, 403–5). In the early years of the gas industry, fears of explosion were much exaggerated, and early gasholders were housed in brick buildings – although ironically this increased the risk, as gas could accumulate between the exterior of the holder and the walls, and bricks became lethal projectiles in an explosion. Early gasholders were also limited in capacity to 6000 cubic feet (170m³) (Stewart 1958, 32). When representatives of a government committee investigating safety visited the Gas Light and Coke's Westminster Works in 1814, they were shocked when the engineer Samuel Clegg punctured a gasholder and put a flame to the escaping gas. To the committee's relief (and as Clegg knew) there was no explosion. The restrictive legislation that the gas industry feared at the time did not materialise (Everard 1949, 59–60).

In the Commercial's district, an explosion at the premises of Mr Abrahams, a baker in Spitalfields, was caused by the Company's main passing over his oven (LMA, B/CGC/2, 101 (26 May 1848)). An explosion on Church Street, Bethnal Green, was blamed on men from the Metropolitan Board of Works disturbing a main during the construction of a sewer (LMA, B/CGC/5, 111 (30 May 1862)). One person was injured by an explosion in High Street, Whitechapel (LMA, B/CGC/8, 85 (10 March 1871)), and another explosion took place in Limehouse at the home of a Mr Philip Swan, who took a lighted candle into his cellar where there was a gas leak (LMA, B/CGC/12, 18 (15 June 1877)).

The advent of steamrollers caused problems for all the gas companies (Everard 1949, 215), and the Commercial was no exception. The roads were in poor repair, potholed and eroded by the weather; often the mains were near the surface and easily broken by heavy machinery. In 1896 a steamroller fractured one of the Company's mains and caused an explosion that injured a passer-by (LMA, B/CGC/17, 125 (19 November 1896)).

Explosions at the Stepney Works itself were not unknown. In 1856, five men were injured when a lighted burner, which one of them was holding, ignited gas escaping from a nearby purifier (*J Gas Sup*, 29 April 1856, 259). In the same year there was a major mains fracture when an accident at the entrance gate of the West India Docks broke the main supplying the Isle of Dogs; fortunately it was not accompanied by an explosion. Before a new main laid across the entrance to the docks on the bed of the river could be completed, a temporary main had to be laid across the bridge, its connections repeatedly having to be broken to allow vessels in and out of the docks (Maddocks 1931, 175).

6.2 Impact on the private domain

The bulk of the Company's trade came from shops, public houses and other public buildings for the first part of its history, and it was only towards the end of the 19th century that gas became available for use in the poorer homes of the district. Prepayment penny-in-the-slot meters were an important innovation. These were developed in 1889 by Thorp and Marsh

(Stewart 1958, 46), and from 1893 the Commercial, like other gas companies, was rapidly widening its clientele to the working class. The engineer submitted a plan for the use of such meters in 1893, and this was carried out later that year (LMA, B/CGC/16, 341 (18 May 1893)). The Company also allowed people to pay for gas in instalments, which helped the poor (*J Gas Sup*, 5 April 1887, 622). Between 1890 and 1910, the extension of the gas supply to all sections of the population resulted in a doubling of the amount of gas sold (Stewart 1958, 47).

For the few affluent households that could afford it, gas was initially charged by the number of burners in the property, with strict limits on when gas could be used. These limits were enforced by Inspectors of Light, who would tour the district on the lookout for illicit gas use. Sometimes companies would receive anonymous tip-offs from neighbours (eg NGA, NT, COG/A/C/1, 14 October 1840). Any consumers found to be breaking their agreement with the Company risked prosecution. The earliest burners were formed as holes in pipe caps, known by such names as 'rat-tail', 'cockspur' or 'cockscomb', according to the shape of flame produced. Later improvements included the batswing burner of 1816, developed after sawcuts replaced holes, and the Argand burner, originally a lamp for burning oil, which was adapted for gas lighting in 1820 (Trueman 1997, 25) (Fig 70).

Like other gas companies, the Commercial quickly realised that it was easier to measure gas use with a meter, and metered gas was made cheaper to encourage its adoption. The two types of meter were 'wet' and 'dry'. Wet meters were inferior to dry ones, as the water could freeze in winter, and a dishonest consumer could obtain more gas by punching a hole in the case and letting out some of the water. Meters became reliable enough for general adoption in 1824 (Everard 1949, 101) and the first satisfactory dry meters were produced from about 1840 (ibid, 105). The Commercial's meters were manufactured by William Smith of Snow Hill, London, from about 1841 (LMA, B/CGC/1, 428 (29 July 1846)). 'Defries' dry meters' were being used by the Company in 1846 (ibid, 326 (18 February 1846)) and were 'in extensive use' across the metropolis by the 1860s (Clegg 1866, 332). The Company also used dry meters 'of Messrs Croll and Glover manufacture' (LMA, B/CGC/1, 574 (17 February 1847)). Croll had set up a factory to make his meters just south of the Canal Bridge in Kingsland Road, Hackney (Mills 1999, 111). Metered gas quickly caught on and by mid 1848 the Company operated at least 3261 meters (LMA, B/CGC/2, 121 (18 August 1848)), of both wet and dry design (ibid, 148 (22 December 1848)). Meters were being repaired on the works by mid 1848 (ibid, 143–6 (15 December 1848)); the work was apparently on quite a small scale and undertaken by one individual, although there was a suggestion that he should be joined by another (ibid, 312 (29 January 1851)). Meters that could not be repaired on site were sent out for repair (LMA, B/CGC/3, 348 (10 February 1854)) and by 1860 a meter rental department had been established (LMA, B/CGC/4, np (3 February 1860)). The meter shop and proving room grew to become an important part of the works, providing assembly, testing and repair (Fig 71; Fig 72).

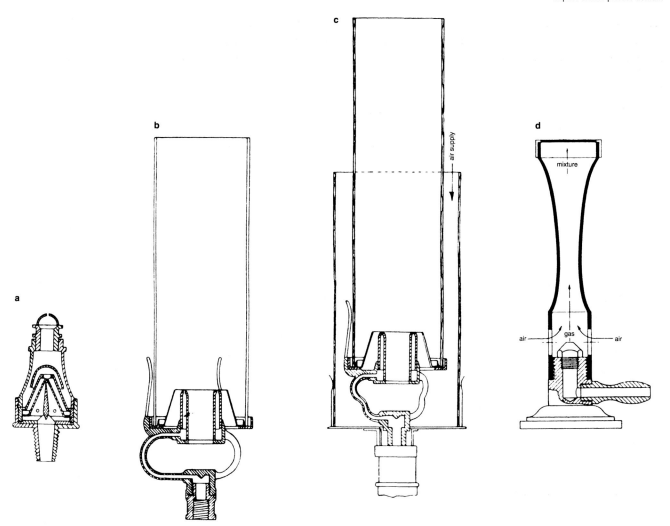

Fig 70 Early domestic gas burners: a – Peebles needle governor burner; b – Sugg's London Argand burner; c – regenerative Argand burner; d – Bunsen burner (Co-partnership H, *October 1934, 178–80*)

Houses in the 19th century would have been very dark to modern eyes, but at the time the use of gas would have transformed the domestic setting, even though in the first part of the century only three or four burners would have been used. Later developments were to have a greater effect, and would help gas companies fend off the threat from electric light. The incandescent mantle burner produced by Welsbach in 1887 secured the maximum of light from a meshed mantle of thorium with a small amount of cerium. Incandescent burner lights differed significantly from their predecessors in that they relied not on the illuminating power of the gas, but on its heating power. There were further improvements in 1900 with the introduction of the inverted mantle burner, which had a higher light efficiency and better light distribution. A few years later the mantle burner had ousted direct flame lighting (Stewart 1958, 46–7).

Traditionally, food would have been prepared on a range, but by the middle of the 19th century gas was beginning to be used for cooking. Gas cooking received celebrity endorsement early in the century; from 1841 the famous chef Alexis Soyer was cooking regularly with gas at the London Reform Club (Stewart 1958, 45). Gas cookers were devised by Croll in 1847

and by Ricketts in 1849. The cookers of King of Liverpool, Sharp of Southampton, and Goddard of Ipswich – all produced in 1850 – were the forerunners of the modern gas cooker (ibid). The Commercial's board was evidently interested in this development, and in 1850 agreed to view 'three Gas Cooking Apparatus of different description' made by Thompson and Sons (LMA, B/CGC/2, 249 (17 April 1850)) and one of a Mr Grant's 'Gas Stoves' (ibid, 261 (5 June 1850)).

By the 1880s a significant number of gas consumers were using gas for at least part of their cooking needs. From this time onwards, gas companies not only supplied lighting, but provided gas and appliances for cooking (Fig 73), space heating, water heating and power (Stewart 1958, 46). The black cast iron cooker gave way to enamelled cast iron around 1913 and eventually to enamelled pressed sheet steel. By 1919 the Company was renting out 22,000 gas stoves (LMA, B/CGC/20, 2 (11 September 1919)); by 1931, this figure had grown to 82,000, with a further 1300 purchased by consumers (*Co-partnership H*, July 1931, 122–5). The thermostat oven was developed in 1923 by Regulo (Stewart 1958, 47) and the Company attempted to boost sales with practical demonstrations of cookery at its showrooms, including

Fig 71 The meter shop as it was in the 1930s (Co-partnership H, October 1935, 192)

Fig 72 The proving room as it was in the 1930s (Co-partnership H, October 1935, 193)

Fig 73 *Gas cookers by Fletcher's of Warrington, hired out by the Commercial Gas Company in the late 19th century: a – Universal Oven; b – Patent Ventilated Hot Air Oven; c – gas cooker (Co-partnership H, July 1931, 122–5)*

'a quickly-prepared dinner for washday' (*Co-partnership H*, November 1934, 205).

Gas for domestic heating was not taken up as quickly as for cooking. The proper means to secure a radiant fire were not understood, and early heaters were flueless even though the gas was impure. Innovations in the middle of the century included the use of pumice balls by Edwards in 1849; Smith and Philips's production of an imitation coal fire using glass and firebrick in 1851; the use of asbestos fibre by Goddard in 1852; and the introduction of the firebrick back in 1859. In 1877 a gas fire was produced with radiants of woven wire (Stewart 1958, 46). Leoni produced a gas fire with tufts of asbestos fibre embedded like a brush in a firebrick back in 1882, and the gas fire with columnar radiants was introduced in 1905 (ibid, 46–7).

Water heaters which crudely applied gas to the underside of a bath were known from 1850, but the first 'geyser' was invented by Maugham in 1868 and successfully improved by Ewart and others (Stewart 1958, 46). Thomas Fletcher improved the design of the instantaneous water heater in 1890, and for the famous 'Africa' gas fire of 1890 – using a metal bracket fitted with skeleton fireclay balls (ibid, 46). Water heaters were further developed by Davis and Potterton in 1904 and by Ascot in 1932, and became boilers linked into central heating (ibid, 47).

7

Conclusions

The Commercial Company and its Stepney Works were transformed as London itself changed. From a tiny gasworks in a virtually rural setting in the 1840s, by the end of the 19th century the works was a complex industrial site in a neighbourhood packed with buildings, and was supplying gas to thousands of consumers, and lighting streets, public buildings, homes and workplaces.

The success of the Company was tied to the expansion of the capital and its ever-growing market of consumers. This success boosted the confidence of a Company that was the first to switch exclusively to clay retorts, and built the world's third largest gasholder in 1864. It also experimented with revivification of metal oxides to aid the purification process.

At the Stepney Works the pace of growth was considerable. Twelve gasholders were built in total, 11 of them in the first 30 years of the Company's existence, an average of one every two and a half years. More would have been built had the works not run out of space. The Company was a major local employer; the manpower and materials needed for the building work alone would have had a significant effect on the local economy.

It was the Company's engineers who had to plan and execute these changes over the years, and the Company was extremely lucky in the engineers it secured, who were responsible not only for the development of the works, but for making sure that enough gas was generated and delivered to consumers.

The steadying hand of the board was crucial too. This enabled the Company to face down competition in the early years. The board's perseverance secured contracts from parochial bodies to lay mains after many disappointments. Rivals recognised that the Commercial was a force to be reckoned with. The districting agreement with other companies, crowned by the Act of Incorporation in 1847, firmly established the Company.

The following decade was pivotal. In the 1850s the board invested huge sums in rebuilding the Stepney Works. There was a mounting urgency to complete the reconstruction as quickly as possible. Demand was rising and the Company had inherited the consumers of the British after driving that company from the capital. Although it is not stated in the Company's Minute Books, it must have crossed the minds of the directors that they had bitten off more than they could chew. Two engineers were lost in quick succession, and the board was then lucky to find Robert Jones, who was to be one of the most important engineers in the history of the Company.

It would be a mistake to see the success of the Company as inevitable. For every Commercial, Gas Light and Coke, or South Metropolitan Company, there was a Poplar Company or East London Company that went to the wall. The gas industry could be unforgiving and vicious. The necessity of survival in this environment quickly changed the character of the Commercial. Originally conceived as being run by its consumers, the Commercial became a company that behaved in much the same way as rivals set up on a different basis. Proprietors' meetings were allowed to fall into abeyance and the amount of the minimum share was increased, cutting down the number of smaller investors.

The beginning of the 1850s saw the Battle of Bow Bridge with the Great Central. This pitched battle between hundreds of workers of two putative consumers' companies is often represented in a slightly humorous light (cf Everard 1949, 186; Mills 1999, 108). The image of two gas companies squaring up to each other and the Commercial's secretary being led away by the police does indeed have a faintly ridiculous cast. However, the reality of this incident was a literal fight for survival that involved spilt blood and broken bones. Had the Great Central succeeded in supplying the Commercial's district with cheaper gas, this would have had serious – perhaps fatal – consequences for the Company. It was not a unique event: a few years earlier workmen from the British Company had dug up mains newly laid by the Commercial on Mile End Waste. Gas companies could not be squeamish about resorting to physical violence to ensure their survival.

The industry was built on brute force. From the first day that gas was produced at Stepney in the late 1830s, the retorts at the works were loaded using the physical strength of the stokers, who were only replaced by mechanisation in the early 20th century. It is ironic, then, that it was not until the 1890s that the sons and grandsons of the workers who had defended the Company's interests with their fists in 1850, and whose labour kept the Company going, could light their homes with the gas that they produced.

There were periodic industrial disputes as gas workers became more organised during the 19th century. The most important strike at the Commercial was the London-wide Stokers' Strike of 1872. Despite the determination of the capital's gas workers, the companies won out, with the state intervening on the side of the employers. The treatment of the defeated strikers was not something of which the capital's gas companies – including the Commercial – could be proud. During the next dispute, in 1889, the Company's reaction was more conciliatory, and the victory of the Commercial's gas workers may have boosted the confidence of neighbouring dockers who embarked on their own famous Dock Strike later that year.

This study has provided an insight into how a gas company reacted to an increasing barrage of legislation after the 1860 Metropolis Gas Act, particularly in relation to gas purification. The City of London Gas Act of 1868 in particular prompted structural changes at the works, specifically to the purifiers. Gas companies could struggle with the legislative requirements placed on them: the Commercial's stinging embarrassment in 1884 when its gas fell below the statutory standard would have been out of all proportion to the £2 fine it had to pay.

Another major development in the later 19th and early 20th centuries was the growing threat from the electricity industry. As a result, gas use was diversified beyond lighting to cooking and heating. Initially dismissive of electricity, by the 1930s the Commercial had developed almost a sense of siege as local authorities pushed electricity as the new, clean form of power.

The latter part of the 19th century also saw a consolidation of the gas industry, with amalgamations producing two giant companies – the Gas Light and Coke and the South Metropolitan, each with huge gasworks. There was agonised debate in the Commercial's boardroom about how to react, but eventually the Company stood aside from amalgamation, apparently concerned that proprietors would not benefit. Perhaps this was a reflex response, arising from the Commercial's past as a consumers' company. Nevertheless, the Company reproduced the process in miniature, amalgamating with the Ratcliff Company and building its own large gasworks at Poplar, which eventually superseded the Stepney Works.

The scope of this study unfortunately does not allow a fuller exploration of the history of the Commercial's Poplar Works. This works was a physical expression of the continuing expansion of the Company and the developing ideas about gasworks design of the then engineer, Harry Jones. However, an excellent start on research into Poplar has been made by Tucker (2000) in his examination of its gasholders. The Company's smaller and idiosyncratic works at Wapping would also repay further research.

There is potential for further research into the Company, particularly into the 20th century, as this study has focused primarily on the Victorian era. Many of the people who worked at Stepney would have been local, and tracing individuals identified by this project and elsewhere (for example in the *Co-partnership Herald*) would deepen understanding of the area's history. Further research into the engineering firms that built the Stepney Works and into the companies with whom the Commercial traded would demonstrate the interconnectedness of industry in London and further afield as the Victorian period progressed.

In more general terms, the methods used for this study – the combining of archaeological recording with historical research – can be used for other similar works, if they cannot be preserved. This could be enhanced by the use of suitable equipment, during the demolition phase or earlier, to uncover below-ground foundations and structures, in order to help understand the many buildings on gasworks sites.

If a company can take on the attributes of the major figures who comprised it, then the Commercial belongs to its first chairman, Charles Salisbury Butler, as well as engineers Isaac Mercer and father and son Robert and Harry Jones. But we should not forget that their efforts were supported by the thousands of workers who toiled for the Company over the many years of its existence, a tiny minority of whom are named in this book.

In his classic 1949 account of the Gas Light and Coke Company and the London gas industry, Stirling Everard revealed a talent for summing up the character of a gas company in a few words. This project has shown how the Commercial Company was always ambitious and confident, occasionally ruthless, but unafraid to innovate or follow its own path.

FRENCH AND GERMAN SUMMARIES

Résumé

Elisabeth Lorans

En 2002, le service archéologique du Musée de Londres (MOLA) fut chargé d'entreprendre une étude d'archéologie du bâti de l'usine à gaz du XIXe siècle de Stepney, à Londres de l'Est. Cette usine avait été le principal lieu de production de la Compagnie Commerciale de Gaz, d'Éclairage et de Coke établie en 1837. Les vestiges subsistants dataient des années 1850 au début du XXe siècle et incluaient quatre gazomètres, un transporteur sur rail surélevé et les murs d'enceinte. Cet ouvrage présente les résultats des relevés ainsi qu'une nouvelle recherche documentaire sur l'histoire de la compagnie.

L'usine à gaz était située sur le Canal du Régent pour faciliter la livraison de charbon. Constituée en 1839 d'un petit gazomètre, d'un bâtiment à retortes et d'une station d'épuration, elle a été agrandie jusqu'à inclure cinq grands réservoirs, quatre bâtiments à retortes et tout un ensemble d'installations d'épuration à la fin du siècle. Douze gazomètres furent construits pendant la durée d'existence de l'usine qui approvisionnait en gaz de ville la plus grande partie de l'est de Londres, incluant Stepney, Whitechapel, Bethnal Green, Bow et Poplar.

Les débuts de la société furent un combat pour sa survie face à des rivaux plus puissants. Cependant, dans un délai assez bref, des accords furent conclus pour le partage des zones d'approvisionnement et la société fut accréditée par le Parlement en 1847. Dans les années 1850, l'usine de Stepney fit l'objet de travaux très importants pour satisfaire aux contraintes règlementaires, de plus en plus fortes à partir de 1860, et faire face à la demande croissante d'une capitale en expansion. Les relations de la société avec ses concurrents furent toujours délicates, conduisant parfois à des violences physiques. Il y eut aussi des épisodes sociaux difficiles, notamment en 1872, quand le personnel de l'entreprise prit part à une grande grève à Londres.

La production de gaz à Stepney cessa en 1945 et l'usine fut fermée en 1946. Le site fut alors utilisé comme lieu de stockage de gaz produit ailleurs, d'abord par la société nationalisée du Gaz du Nord de la Tamise puis par ses successeurs jusque dans les années 1990. Depuis, le terrain a été réaménagé pour l'habitat mais un certain nombre d'éléments historiques ont été conservés ou réutilisés dans le projet immobilier.

L'histoire de la Compagnie Commerciale et les transformations de l'usine de Stepney n'avaient pas reçu jusqu'à présent l'attention détaillée qu'elles méritaient. Cette publication restitue à la compagnie sa juste place dans l'histoire de la production de gaz à Londres.

Zusammenfassung

Manuela Struck

Im Jahr 2002 wurde der Archäologische Dienst des Museums of London (MOLA) mit der Bauaufnahme der Stepney-Gaswerke des 19. Jhs. in Ost-London beauftragt. Die Gasfabrik, erbaut

1837, stellte die Hauptanlage der „Commercial Gas Light and Coke Company" dar. Die erhaltenen Reste datierten in die Zeit zwischen den 1850ern Jahren und dem frühen 20. Jh. und umfassten vier Gasbehälter, eine Hochbahnlinie und die Umfassungsmauern. Die vorliegende Publikation präsentiert die Ergebnisse der Bauaufnahme im Rahmen einer neuen dokumentarischen Geschichte der Gesellschaft.

Im Hinblick auf eine reibungslose Belieferung mit Kohle befanden sich die Gaswerke am Regent's-Kanal. Ausgehend von einem kleinen Gasbehälter, einem Retortenhaus und einem Reinigungsgebäude von 1839 wuchsen sie bis zum Ende des Jahrhunderts auf fünf große Gasometer, vier Retortenhäuser und einen ganzen Komplex an Reinigungsanlagen an. Insgesamt wurden zwölf Gasbehälter während der Geschichte der Gasfabrik gebaut. Die Firma belieferte große Teile Ost-Londons mit Stadtgas, inklusive Stepney, Whitechapel, Bethnal Green, Bow und Poplar.

Die ersten Jahre des Betriebs waren gezeichnet vom Überlebenskampf gegen mächtigere Konkurrenten. Innerhalb kurzer Zeit traf man jedoch Vereinbarungen über die Absatzgebiete, und die Gesellschaft wurde 1847 durch eine Parlamentsakte offiziell als Gesellschaft etabliert. In den 1850er Jahren wurde die Anlage von Stepney einem größeren Bauprogramm unterzogen, um eine stabile Firmenbasis zu schaffen, die der komplizierteren Gesetzgebung von 1860 und der steigenden Nachfrage der wachsenden Hauptstadt gerecht wurde. Das Verhältnis der Gesellschaft zu ihren Konkurrenten war immer reizbar, was manchmal sogar zu physischer Gewalt führte. Es gab auch Episoden der Unruhe seitens der Arbeiter, speziell 1872, als sich die Belegschaft der Firma den londonweiten Streiks anschloss.

Die Gasproduktion in Stepney endete 1945, und die Werke wurden 1946 geschlossen. Das Gelände wurde dann bis in die 1990er Jahre als Gasometer-Station (zur Lagerung von Gas, das andernorts produziert worden war) vom verstaatlichten „North Thames Gas Board" und deren Nachfolgern genutzt. Danach erfuhr das Gebiet eine Sanierung und Umgestaltung zur Wohnfläche, wobei eine Anzahl historischer Elemente beibehalten oder innerhalb der Bebauung wiederbenutzt wurde.

Bis heute ist der Geschichte der Gesellschaft und der Entwicklung der Stepney Werke nicht die detaillierte Aufmerksam zuteil geworden, die sie verdienen. Diese Publikation verschafft der Gesellschaft nun ihren rechtmäßigen Platz innerhalb der Geschichte der Londoner Gasindustrie.

BIBLIOGRAPHY

Manuscript sources

London Metropolitan Archives (LMA)

B/CGC Commercial Gas Light and Coke Company, minutes of directors' meetings (NB there is a gap in the records between March 1855 and November 1856); references to the Minute Books in the text are in the form (B/CGC/1, 22 (10 April 1844)), indicating the particular Minute Book, page number (where given, otherwise 'np') and date of the meeting referred to

B/CGC/1 (10 April 1844–16 June 1847)
B/CGC/2 (23 June 1847–14 November 1851)
B/CGC/3 (21 November 1851–16 March 1855)
B/CGC/4 (21 November 1856–29 June 1860)
B/CGC/5 (6 July 1860–15 July 1864)
B/CGC/6 (22 July 1864–25 June 1869)
B/CGC/7 (index to B/CGC/6)
B/CGC/8 (2 July 1869–10 October 1873)
B/CGC/9 (index to B/CGC/8)
B/CGC/10 (17 October 1873–4 May 1877)
B/CGC/11 (index to B/CGC/10)
B/CGC/12 (11 May 1877–21 November 1879)
B/CGC/13 (28 November 1879–29 September 1882)
B/CGC/14 (6 October 1882–19 March 1886)
B/CGC/15 (26 March 1886–27 September 1889)
B/CGC/16 (4 October 1889–14 March 1895)
B/CGC/17 (21 March 1895–1 October 1903)
B/CGC/18 (15 October 1903–27 November 1913)
B/CGC/19 (11 December 1913–28 August 1919)
B/CGC/20 (11 September 1919–23 July 1925)
B/CGC/21 (6 August 1925–14 July 1932)
B/CGC/22 (28 July 1932–29 September 1938)
B/CGC/23 (13 October 1938–28 April 1949)

SC/GL/GOA/VOL/XII/1891, 378 Goad insurance map 1891 [held at Guildhall Library]

National Grid Archive (formerly National Gas Archive) (NGA)

FORMER NORTH THAMES GAS BOARD AND PREDECESSORS

NT, COG/A/C/1 file of miscellaneous correspondence: two letters to Ratcliff Gas Company (14 October 1840 and 3 December 1841) re mains laying; notes on supply of gas to defaulting tenants (1880); letters from auditor re purchase of gas from Amonial Charcoal Co (1882–3)

NT, COG/E/A/1 elevation of buildings facing the canal and proposed alterations (retort house, cross house and coal store, Stepney) (nd, but c 1870)

NT, COG/E/P/1 volume of specifications for gas holders at Stepney (1892–1938): specifications for heightening gasholders 2 and 3 [IX and X] (February–April 1892); specifications for new gasholder 4 [XII] (March 1925); specifications for the repair of gasholder 1 [XI] (May 1931); specifications for the repair of gasholder 2 [IX] (26 June 1935)

NT, COG/E/T/2 *Stepney. Alterations and additions to guide framing of no. 2 & no. 3 gas holders* (detail of new column in guide frames, collars and girders to gasholders 2 and 3 [**IX** and **X**]) (February–April 1892)

NT, COG/E/T/7 *Elevation of no. 1* [**XI**] *holder as altered 1885 (Stepney Works)* (nd)

NT, COG/X/X/1 *To the consumers of gas of the Commercial Gas Company* (leaflet from directors to customers, *c* December 1849)

Tower Hamlets Local History Library and Archives (LBTH)

L/SGE/J/4/30 (shelfmark STE/662/4) Records of the St George-in-the-East paving commissioners – correspondence with the Commercial Gas Light and Coke Company, 1840

Printed and other secondary works

Bar-Niv, Z H (ed), 1979 *International labour law reports: Vol 2*, Alphen aan den Rijn

Ball, M, and Sunderland, D, 2001 *An economic history of London 1800–1914*, London

The Builder, 1851 Gas works, Stepney, *The Builder* 9, 14 June, 380

Cherry, B, O'Brian, C, and Pevsner, N, 2005 *London 5: East*, Buildings of England, London

Clegg, S, 1853 (1841) *A practical treatise on the manufacture and distribution of coal gas*, 2 edn, London

Clegg, S, 1859 (1841) *A practical treatise on the manufacture and distribution of coal gas*, 3 edn, London

Clegg, S, 1866 (1841) *A practical treatise on the manufacture and distribution of coal gas*, 4 edn, London

Colburn, Z, 1865 *The gasworks of London*, London

Cole, G D H, Beer, M, and Maccoby, S, 2002 *Routledge library of British political history: labour and radical politics 1762–1937*, London

Co-partnership H The Co-partnership Herald (1930–6) (magazine produced by the Commercial Gas Light and Coke Company; consulted at LBTH)

Cross, J, 1847 (1837) *Cross's pocket plan of London and street directory*, 3 edn, London

Everard, S, 1949 *The history of the Gas Light and Coke Company, 1812–1949*, London

Galenson, D W, 1994 The rise of free labor, in *Capitalism in context: essays on economic development and cultural change in honor of R M Hartwell* (eds J A James and M Thomas), 114–37, Chicago

Gibson, A V, 1958 Huguenot weavers' houses in Spitalfields, *East London Papers* 1, 3–14

Giles, C, and Goodall, I, 1992 *Yorkshire textile mills 1770–1930*, London

Glendee, 2004 Pictorial record of constructional features: demolition of four column guided gasholders at Stepney, London, unpub Glendee (UK) Ltd rep

Glenny Crory, W, 1876 *East London industries*, London

Greenwood, C, and Greenwood, J, 1827 'Map of London from an Actual Survey', reproduced in Margary 1982, *'Map of London from an Actual Survey' by C and J Greenwood, 1827*, Margary in assoc Guildhall Library, Kent

Jones, H E, 1875 The construction of gasworks, *Min Proc ICE* 40, 2–59

J Gas Sup Journal of Gas Lighting, Water Supply and Sanitary Improvements (1856–1908) (consulted at NGA)

Lewey, F R, 1944 *Cockney campaign*, London

Maddocks, S, 1931 [early history of the Commercial Gas Light and Coke Company] *The Co-partnership Herald* 1, 22–4 (March 1931); 38–41 (April 1931); 62–6 (May 1931); 87–90 (June 1931); 115–19 (July 1931); 140–3 (August 1931); 172–6 (September 1931); 188–91 (October 1931); 221–4 (November 1931)

Mechanics Mag, 1840 Ascent of the Nassau Balloon, *Mechanics Magazine, Museum, Register, Journal and Gazette* 896, 10 October, 384

Mills, M, 1999 *The early east London gas industry and its waste products: how were they used?*, London

Mills, M, 2004 The gas workers' strike in south London, *Greenwich Industrial Hist* 7(1), http://gihs.gold.ac.uk/gihs35.html (accessed November 2009)

Richards, W, 1877 *A practical treatise on the manufacture and distribution of coal gas*, London

Ridge, T, 1998 Commercial gasworks, unpub rep

Rocque, J, 1746 'Exact Survey of the City of London Westminster and Southwark and the Country 10 Miles Round', reproduced in Margary, H, 1971 *'Exact Survey of the City of London Westminster and Southwark and the Country 10 Miles Round' by John Rocque, 1746*, Margary in assoc Guildhall Library, Kent

Schmiechen, J A, 1984 *Sweated industries and sweated labour: the London clothing trades 1860–1914*, London

Skempton, A W (ed), 2001 *A biographical dictionary of civil engineers in Great Britain and Ireland: Vol 1, 1500–1830*, London

Stanford, E, 1862 'Stanford's Library Map of London', reproduced in Margary, H, 1980 *'Stanford's Library Map of London, 1862'*, Margary in assoc Guildhall Library, Kent

Stewart, E G, 1957 *Historical index of gasworks past and present in the area now served by the North Thames Gas Board, 1806–1957*, London

Stewart, E G, 1958 *Town gas: its manufacture and distribution*, London

Sturt, B, 1980 Low pressure gas storage, *London's Industrial Archaeol* 2, 13–23

Taylor, G L, 1848 *On gas works and the introduction of cannel coal gas (thoroughly purified) into the metropolis*, London

Tristan, F, 1982 (1842) *The London journal of Flora Tristan, 1842, or, The aristocracy and the working class of England* (trans J Hawkes), London

Trueman, M R G, 1997 English Heritage Monuments Protection Programme gas industry step 1 report, unpub Lancaster Univ Archaeol Unit rep

Tucker, M T, 2000 London gasholders survey: the development of the gasholder in London in the later nineteenth century, unpub English Heritage rep

Tyler, K, 1999 The former Commercial Gasworks, Harford Street: an industrial heritage assessment, unpub MOL rep

Tyler, K, 2002 The former Commercial Gasworks, Harford Street, London E1: method statement for the recording of standing structures, unpub MOL rep

Tyler, K, 2004 The former Commercial Gasworks, Harford Street, London E1: method statement for the recording of standing structures, unpub MOL rep

Tyler, K, 2005 The former Commercial Gasworks, Ben Jonson Road/Harford Street, London E1: a survey of standing structures, unpub MOL rep

Weightman, G, and Humphries, S, 1983 *The making of modern London 1815–1914*, London

Weller, R, nd [1858] *Postal map of London compiled and engraved by Richard Weller showing the postal districts in 1858*, National Postal Museum facsimile edn, London

INDEX

Compiled by Ann Hudson

Page numbers in **bold** indicate illustrations and maps
All street names and locations are in London unless specified otherwise
County names within parentheses refer to historic counties